NATIONAL
GEOGRAPHIC
KiDS

CAPTAIN AQUATICA'S
AWESOME OCEAN

Amazing Animals!
Wild Waves!
Super Sharks!
The Deep Sea!

Jess Cramp
With Grace Hill Smith and Joe Levit

Science *SUPERHEROES*

CONTENTS

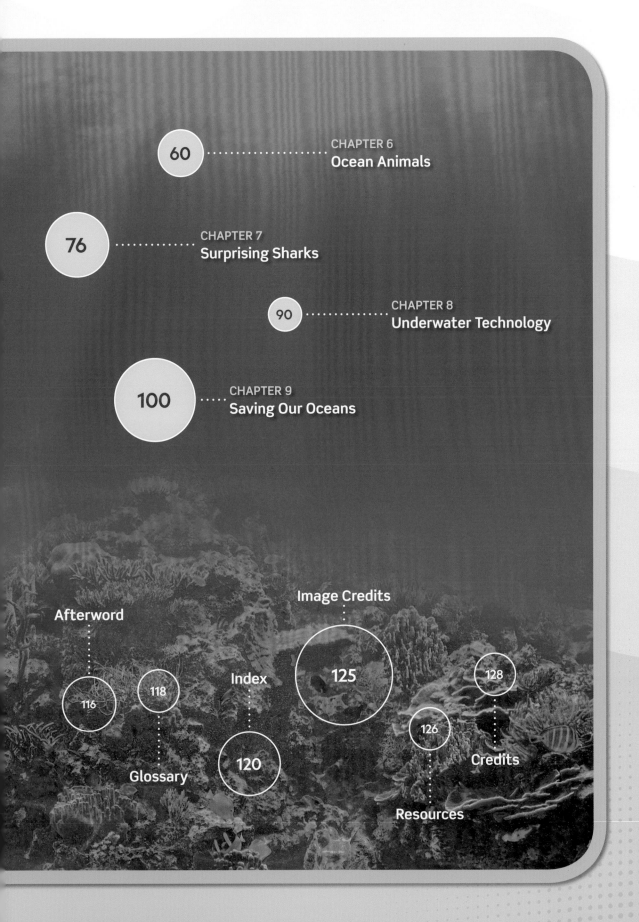

Kia Orana!

MY NAME IS JESS CRAMP and I'm a shark researcher, marine conservationist, and National Geographic Explorer. "Kia Orana" is how we greet our friends here in the Cook Islands, which is the beautiful island nation that is currently both my home and research base. I am writing to you from the mountainous island of Rarotonga, the most populated of the 15 islands that make up the Cook Islands. We're located in the middle of the great big blue South Pacific Ocean.

While I love and respect all the creatures in the ocean, my research focuses on sharks and how best to protect them. This is only possible, though, if I consider the greater ocean ecosystem. Yes, I'm talking about the fish, squid, and plankton that sharks like to eat, but also the ocean as a whole and the people who rely on the ocean as a resource for food, work, and fun.

Sharks have been on the planet for over 400 million years—that's longer than the dinosaurs! But despite the millions of years of evolution and resilience by sharks, human activities in recent decades have put many shark populations in big trouble.

Protecting sharks isn't easy. Tens of millions of sharks and rays are killed every year for their fins, meat, liver oil, gill plates, and other parts. In addition to fishing for their parts, they also face many threats, such as climate change, habitat destruction, and pollution, all of which we'll talk about in this book. And not everyone likes sharks. Some people naturally fear sharks because they think they are a threat. Fears are also caused by inaccurate depictions of sharks in movies and media. Then there are real-life frustrations faced by people who rely on the ocean. For example, fishermen here in the Cook Islands and in other island nations feel frustrated when sharks steal tuna off of their fishing lines—tuna that the fishermen need to feed and support their families.

Jess Cramp tagging sharks in the Cook Islands

Jess Cramp's research boat surrounded by Sharks.

By working with fishermen, we can learn a lot. But we can also teach—and lead by example. We can help people learn about these animals and the ocean. We can teach people that sharks and the entire ocean are important, and that many animal species and the ocean itself are in trouble. I love involving the local communities in my research. Working with communities is important to turn research into meaningful protection for sharks, other marine life, and the waters they call home. In fact, I teamed up with fishermen, farmers, growers, dancers, voyagers, and politicians here to create the Cook Islands Shark Sanctuary in 2012. In the sanctuary, an area of water that is three times the size of Texas, U.S.A., it's illegal for commercial boats to fish for sharks, rays, skates, or chimaeras (a relative of sharks). If any of these animals are caught, they must be returned to the ocean. It's also illegal to possess any shark part or to import, export, sell, or transport sharks.

That's just some of what I do in real life. In this book, though, you'll see me as the superscientist, Captain Aquatica. My finntastic (but sometimes nervous!) hammerhead sidekick, Finn, and I will ride ocean currents around the world, braving supersize storms and traveling through undersea mountain ranges. We'll visit different ocean zones and undersea ecosystems, use top underwater technology, and meet the many awesome animals that call the ocean their home, including super sharks—all on our mission to save these spectacular species and protect the spectacular ocean.

The comics in this book, like the superhero Captain A, are fictional, of course. But the science is real. Are you ready to dive in?

OUR AMAZING OCEAN

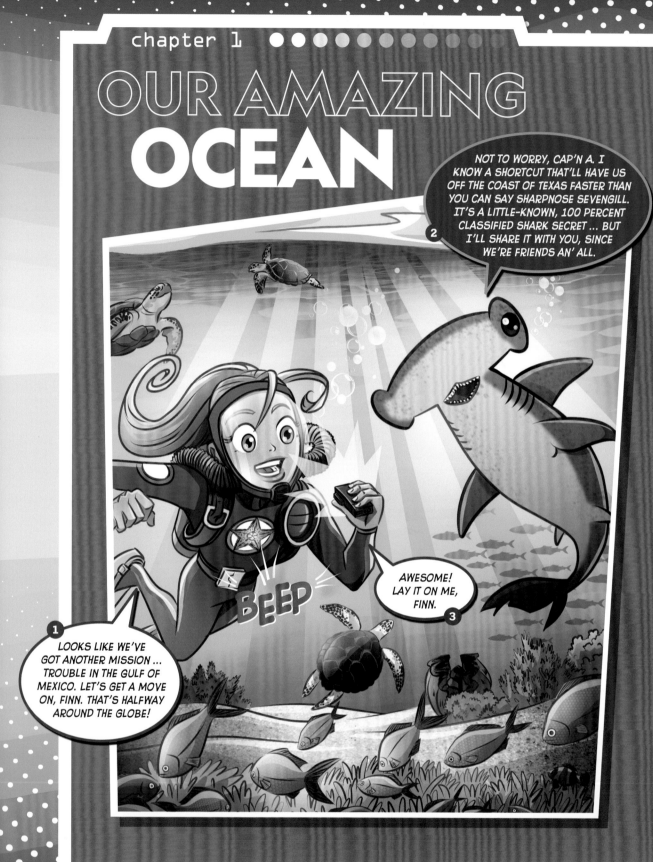

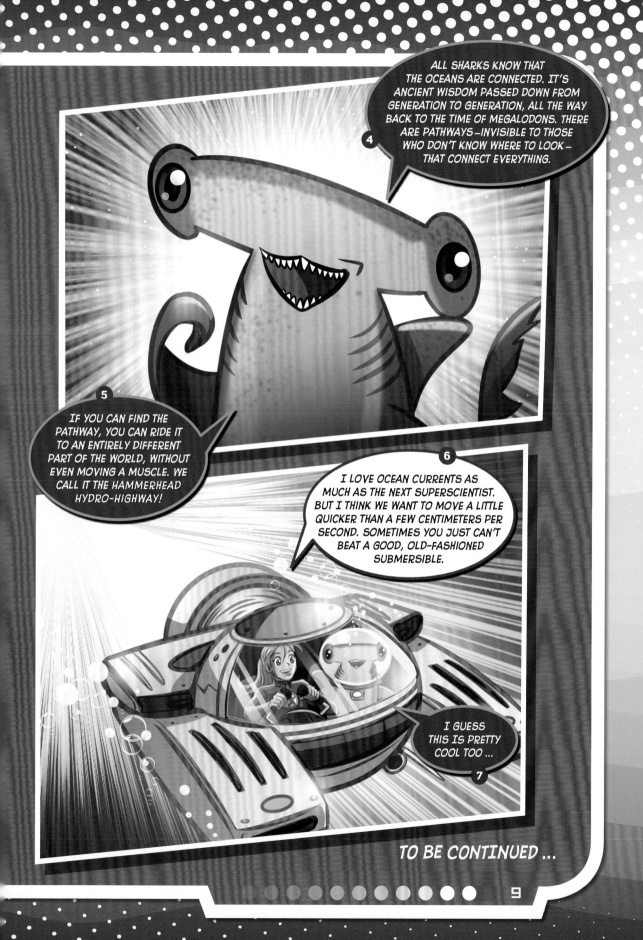

TO BE CONTINUED ...

OUR AMAZING OCEAN

Seen from outer space, the Earth looks like a giant blue marble. That is because the deep blue ocean covers about three-quarters of our planet's surface. It is so vast that humans have explored only about 20 percent of its watery depths. There's a lot left to be discovered!

THE WORLD OCEAN

This huge single body of water is divided up into four smaller oceans named the Pacific, Atlantic, Indian, and Arctic. Some oceanographers consider the icy waters surrounding Antarctica to be a fifth ocean called the Southern or Antarctic Ocean. The borders of these oceans are formed by continents, groups of islands, and features of the ocean floor, such as underwater mountain ranges. Each ocean has its own characteristics. Differences in temperature, geology, and salinity (how salty the water is) make each one unique.

Combined, the four oceans contain about 97 percent of the world's water. The other 3 percent is frozen in glaciers and ice caps; is found in bodies of freshwater such as lakes, ponds, and rivers; falls as rainwater; or exists as water vapor in the atmosphere.

THE PACIFIC OCEAN

The Pacific Ocean is the largest ocean. It spans an area of 69 million square miles (178.8 sq km) and contains almost half of Earth's ocean water. More than 25,000

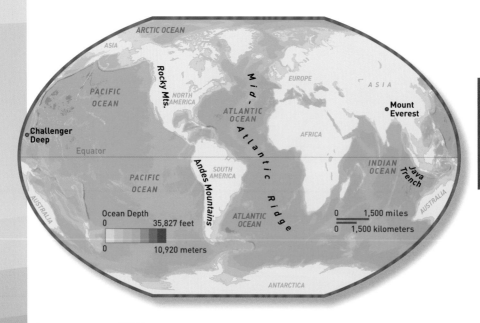

ARCTIC OCEAN

ASIA

EUROPE

ASIA

Rocky Mts.

NORTH AMERICA

PACIFIC OCEAN

Mid-Atlantic Ridge

ATLANTIC OCEAN

AFRICA

• Mount Everest

• Challenger Deep

Equator

Andes Mountains

SOUTH AMERICA

INDIAN OCEAN

Java Trench

PACIFIC OCEAN

ATLANTIC OCEAN

AUSTRALIA

AUSTRALIA

Ocean Depth
0   35,827 feet
0   10,920 meters

0   1,500 miles
0   1,500 kilometers

ANTARCTICA

Earth's nickname is the blue planet for a reason: Oceans cover 75 percent of it. This map shows how the four oceans connect.

Satellite images show typhoon Haiyan swirling over the South China Sea in 2013. It was one of the strongest typhoons ever recorded.

islands dot its surface. All the world's continents combined could fit inside its basin. The Mariana Trench, a canyon more than 1,500 miles (2,414 km) long, cuts across the western Pacific seafloor. Challenger Deep, the deepest point on Earth, is found in this crescent-shaped trench. It plunges nearly seven miles (11.3 km) below the ocean's surface.

Thousands of people have summited Mount Everest, the highest point on Earth, but only three people have descended to Challenger Deep.

The famous Portuguese navigator Ferdinand Magellan named the Pacific Ocean, which means "peaceful." Its waters, he said, seemed calm after a rough trip west across the Atlantic Ocean. But the Pacific is not always as Magellan described. Its warm temperatures help create typhoons (another name for hurricanes, used when these storms are in the Indian or western Pacific Oceans). Around the edges of the Pacific Basin is the Ring of Fire, called this because it is dotted with about two-thirds of Earth's

TEMPERATURES VARY ACROSS THE VAST PACIFIC OCEAN. IN THE SOUTH PACIFIC, WATERS ARE ABOUT 80°F (26°C). IN THE NORTH PACIFIC, WATERS CAN BE AS COOL AS 28.6°F (1.9°C).

active volcanoes and causes 90 percent of all earthquakes (see p. 35). These earthquakes and volcanic eruptions can also cause tsunamis, which are sometimes damaging waves that can reach some hundred feet (30 m) high.

NORTH
AMERICA

ASIA

Strait of
Gibraltar
EUROPE

AFRICA

THE STRAIT OF GIBRALTAR AS SEEN
FROM SPACE. TO THE WEST (LEFT) IS
THE ATLANTIC OCEAN. TO THE EAST
(RIGHT) IS THE MEDITERRANEAN SEA.

PASS THE SALT

According to some scientists, warming temperatures have caused the water
in the Mediterranean Sea to get saltier. This increased salinity, or saltiness, is
because the amount of water evaporating—leaving the sea and mixing with
the air—is greater than the amount of rain replenishing it. And since salt does
not evaporate, the sea has the same amount of salt but less water.

So if more water is evaporating and not raining back down, what keeps
the Mediterranean Sea from drying up? The Mediterranean is almost
completely surrounded by land: Europe to the north, Africa to the south, and
the Middle East to the east. But the Strait of Gibraltar to the west connects
the Mediterranean with the Atlantic. The strait might be narrow, but this
waterway has two strong currents that allow water from the ocean and the sea
to mix. One current flows the Atlantic water eastward into the Mediterranean,
and the other flows the Mediterranean water underneath it westward into the
Atlantic. So the Mediterranean shares some of its salt with the Atlantic, while
the less salty Atlantic water replenishes the Mediterranean Basin.

A statue of the Greek god Atlas, from whom the Atlantic Ocean gets its name, shows the titan holding the world on his shoulders.

The Atlantic Ocean has another defining feature: the Mid-Atlantic Ridge, a chain of undersea mountains 10,000 miles (16,000 km) long. About four times as long as the Himalaya, the Andes, and the Rocky Mountains combined, the Mid-Atlantic Ridge is the world's longest mountain range. Some mountaintops peek out of the water to form islands, such as Iceland and the Azores.

THE INDIAN OCEAN

The Indian Ocean is named after the country that juts out into its waters. It has the fewest trenches of any of the world's oceans, but it has the second longest one: The Java Trench slices through some 2,000 miles (3,200 km) of seafloor. The tropical waters of the Indian Ocean are also home to the largest breeding ground for humpback whales, which travel as many as 4,000 miles (6,400 km) from their feeding areas in Antarctica. And a creature once thought to be extinct for 66 million years swims here too. The coelacanth, a species of fish, was found living in the waters between the African island of Madagascar and the African country of Mozambique in 1938.

THE ATLANTIC OCEAN

The Atlantic Ocean is named after Atlas, a titan from Greek mythology who was believed to carry the whole world on his shoulders. This ocean was the first to be crossed by both ship and airplane. Second only to the Pacific in size, it contains the world's largest island—Greenland. (And "green" this island is not—about 80 percent of it is covered in ice!)

The ocean can hold surprises. The coelacanth, which was once thought to be extinct and was known only from fossils, was found in the waters off Madagascar in Africa.

Walruses are just some of the many animals that make their home among the sea ice in the Arctic Ocean.

THE ARCTIC OCEAN

The Arctic Ocean is the smallest and north-ernmost ocean on Earth. It is nearly land-locked by Alaska, U.S.A.; Canada; Greenland; Norway; Finland; Sweden; and Russia. Only the small Greenland and Norwegian Seas and the even smaller Bering Strait connect it to the larger ocean. The Arctic Ocean is partially cov-ered with ice year-round. During the winter, ice covers nearly the whole ocean. "Ocean" may seem like the wrong word for a body of water that can freeze into ice 12 to 15 feet (4 to 5 m) thick. Indeed, it is land to many animals that make their home on this ice- and snow-packed tip of the world. Walruses give birth to their young on the sea ice, and seals dive under it to catch fish—or to escape the polar bears that hunt them.

CONNECTED BY CURRENTS

The Pacific, Atlantic, Indian, and Arctic Oceans are all interconnected. How? Through cur-rents, which transport vast amounts of water from one place to another. They move around the entire globe, both at the ocean's surface and deeper underwater.

Surface currents are driven by strong winds that blow against the water's surface, dragging water along with the wind. These currents flow like rivers, carrying warm water from the sun-drenched tropics to the frigid North and South Poles, and cold water from the polar regions to the tropics. The Gulf Stream, for example, is a swift current in the Atlantic Ocean that begins in the Caribbean

THE GULF STREAM TRANSPORTS ALMOST FOUR BILLION CUBIC FEET (113 MILLION CUBIC M) OF WATER PER SECOND. THAT IS MORE WATER THAN ALL THE WORLD'S RIVERS COMBINED CAN MOVE IN THE SAME AMOUNT OF TIME.

and brings warm water up from the Gulf of Mexico, past the lower part of the East Coast of the United States. From there it heads northeast toward Europe, where its warm waters help heat the air. This keeps tempera-tures in northern European countries warmer than in other countries that are at the same lat-itude, or the same distance from the Equator.

A heat map of ocean surface tempera-tures shows the Gulf Stream, which carries warm water, in red.

RISING TO THE TOP

Along coastlines, the Coriolis effect causes winds to push warmer surface water away from the shore. Currents of cold water then rise, or well up, to take that water's place. This process is called upwelling. These rising waters bring with them nutrients from below, the bits of food and waste from the creatures above that have sunk to the bottom. One of the best known areas of upwelling occurs off the coast of Chile in South America (La Portada Natural Monument, part of the Chilean coast, is pictured here.) Plankton, which are tiny plants and animals, feed on these nutrients from the seafloor, creating an amazing fishing ground. Small fish feed on the plankton, and larger fish feed on the smaller fish.

Upwelling occurs in the open ocean near the Equator as well, where northern and southern currents meet, allowing deeper water to come to the surface.

The Gulf Stream transports almost four billion cubic feet (113 million cu m) of water per second. That is more water than all the world's rivers combined can move in that time.

To better understand how surface currents move, let's look at how the Earth itself moves. Our planet spins on its axis from west to east, which makes air move in a curved path. (If the Earth did not rotate, air would circulate between the poles in a straight line.) But because of this rotation, the air veers toward the right in the Northern Hemisphere and to the left in the Southern Hemisphere. This deflection, or veering, of air is called the Coriolis effect. This phenomenon also affects surface currents, which follow these same curved paths in each hemisphere.

NAMED SURFACE CURRENTS

The Coriolis effect also creates the strong winds that sailors have used for centuries to speed their journeys. They're called tradewinds because they often helped trade—transporting goods from one place to another. People have identified and named certain surface currents they've used to explore different parts of our planet or to transport goods.

Flowing southwest through the Atlantic Ocean is the Canary Current. It transports cool water south along the west coast of Africa, cooling the Sahara to the east.

At the southern end of Africa is the Agulhas Current. The Agulhas Current cruises along the southeastern coast of Mozambique and South Africa, and then flows east toward Australia, traveling at up to 1.4 miles an hour (2.2 km/h).

UNDERNEATH THE SURFACE

Although you can't see it, the ocean is in constant motion beneath the surface too. These movements of water are called subsurface currents. They are bigger and move much more slowly than currents on the surface.

They are not driven by winds but by differences in water density. Variations in temperature and salinity (how salty the water is) affect the water's density.

Warm water rises and cold water sinks because cold water is more dense than warm water. How does this work? Picture a group of penguins huddling together on the ice to stay warm. Similar to those Antarctic birds, cold-water molecules squeeze together, allowing more molecules to fit in a smaller space. Like the snow in a snowball (see sidebar on p. 18), the molecules are more tightly packed. In contrast, warm-water molecules, moving fast in response to a heat source (like the sun, for example), bounce away from each other. This increases the space between the molecules and thus decreases the water's density.

Salty water is more dense than less salty water, so it sinks too. Why? Because as salt dissolves in water, it increases the water's mass, or weight, so a cup of salt water is heavier than a cup of freshwater.

This constant rising and sinking of cold and warm water, salty and less salty water, is part of a system called the global ocean conveyor

SCIENTIST PROFILE

Benjamin Franklin

The Gulf Stream was discovered by Spanish explorer Juan Ponce de León in 1513, who wrote that this ocean current seemed to be stronger than the wind. It wasn't mapped until the 1770s, when American statesman and inventor Benjamin Franklin asked his cousin and ship captain Timothy Folger why it took him less time to sail to the American Colonies than it did for Franklin's mail ships. Folger knew about the warm, strong current that shaved time off of long Atlantic crossings, and sketched for his cousin the location of this "river in the ocean," as Franklin had described it. Franklin distributed the map to British mariners. When the American Revolution began, however, Franklin ceased sharing his stream secrets. He gave copies to the French instead, who used the information to get supplies and weapons to the Colonies more quickly.

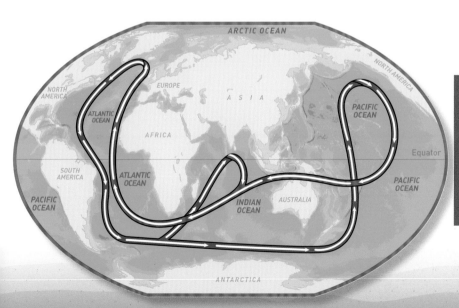

The global ocean conveyor belt helps move water around the world. The blue line shows the movement of cold, salty, deep ocean water. The red shows the movement of warmer surface water.

belt. It moves water in a loop around the world. The global ocean conveyor belt moves through the North Atlantic Ocean. There, cold, salty (and thus dense) water sinks and heads south along the bottom of the Atlantic Basin, toward Antarctica. When it reaches the frigid Antarctic waters, it mixes with even more cold and salty water. It then heads east across the Pacific seafloor (some of it goes up into the Indian Ocean).

When the deep, cold current reaches the North Pacific, it rises to the surface to replace water that winds are pushing away. It warms up and flows as a surface current back to the North Atlantic. It cools, and the journey begins again.

Scientists estimate that 35 cubic feet (1 cubic m) of water—equal to the water in about six bathtubs—travels at just a few centimeters per second. So it will take about a thousand years for that amount of water to complete a full journey through the global ocean conveyor belt.

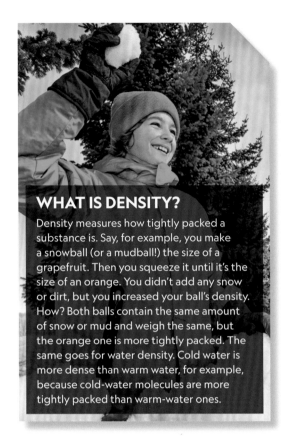

WHAT IS DENSITY?

Density measures how tightly packed a substance is. Say, for example, you make a snowball (or a mudball!) the size of a grapefruit. Then you squeeze it until it's the size of an orange. You didn't add any snow or dirt, but you increased your ball's density. How? Both balls contain the same amount of snow or mud and weigh the same, but the orange one is more tightly packed. The same goes for water density. Cold water is more dense than warm water, for example, because cold-water molecules are more tightly packed than warm-water ones.

TRY THIS
Different Water Density

Saltier water is more dense than less salty water, so it sinks. In the ocean, saltier waters move beneath lighter, less salty waters. This action helps the ocean waters circulate. Try this experiment to see the principle in action.

Materials:
- Egg
- Two small clear bowls
- Water
- Salt
- Whisk

1. Fill one small bowl with lukewarm tap water.

2. Fill the second small bowl with lukewarm tap water, then add 1 cup of salt.

3. Use the whisk to stir the salt water until the salt dissolves.

4. Place the egg into the bowl with plain water. Watch what happens. The egg sinks.

5. Now place the egg into the bowl with salt water. Watch what happens. The egg floats!

What You Learned

If an object is less dense than the water around it, it will float. In this experiment, the egg is less dense than the salt water, so it rises to the surface. This is similar to how less dense warm water rises above more dense cold water in the ocean. In the Dead Sea, which lies between Israel and Jordan, the water is so salty—and thus dense—that people cannot sink in it!

RIDING THE OCEAN'S CURRENTS

Many ocean animals use currents to help them move from one place to another—including sea turtles such as the ones shown here—and ride currents during their migrations. Sharks follow currents for many reasons, including food, and even jellyfish float in currents to get from place to place.

Currents can even transport toy animals. In 1992 a storm in the North Pacific Ocean washed 12 large containers off of a cargo ship. One of the containers held 28,800 plastic bath toys. The toys didn't have holes in them, so they floated along on the local currents. Some yellow ducks ended up in Alaska, some green frogs in Hawaii, U.S.A., and some blue turtles in Australia. A few even spent years frozen in Arctic ice, only to reach Britain or Ireland some 15 years later.

These "Friendly Floatees," as they were nicknamed, became more than just a story about cute bath toys lost at sea. They not only helped scientists learn more about how ocean currents work, but they also provided a startling picture of the global issue of plastic pollution. It takes a long time for plastic to disappear; instead, sun and waves break it down into smaller and smaller pieces. When human trash—including loads of plastic—ends up in the sea, it's picked up by currents and transported all over the world. Plastic threatens sea life. Marine animals eat bits of plastic, which their bodies can't process, and they can get caught in plastic bags.

Bobbing along in their vast ocean bathtub for more than 25 years, the rubber duckies and their fellow floaters raised awareness about just how long—and how much—plastic floats in Earth's oceans.

chapter 2

WAVES, TIDES, AND WILD WEATHER

WAVES, TIDES, AND WILD WEATHER

ave you ever seen a surfer catch a ride on a wave at the beach? She lies on her board, waiting to catch the first swell. Suddenly she is lifted up and forward. *Whee!* The wave brings her down at the shore and then tugs her back into the water just a bit before she jumps up and heads out for another ride.

WHAT ARE WAVES?

Watching that surfer from the beach, it might seem like a huge arc of water is moving from one point in the ocean to the shore, with the surfer as the lucky rider. But the science of waves has a surprise in store: That wave is energy on the move, not water. How is that possible? Let's take a look at where waves come from.

Waves form when wind and water meet at the ocean's surface. When wind blows against surface water, its force causes friction. The friction pushes up some of the water, causing ripples. The wind continues to push the ripples, eventually creating the crest, or top, of a wave. The wind transfers its energy to the wave, and then that energy travels—in that curved swell you know so well—across the water. Unlike surface currents, which are also driven by wind, breaking waves do not move water long distances. The water in a wave actually moves in a circular motion. On the board—or even just bobbing in the water—

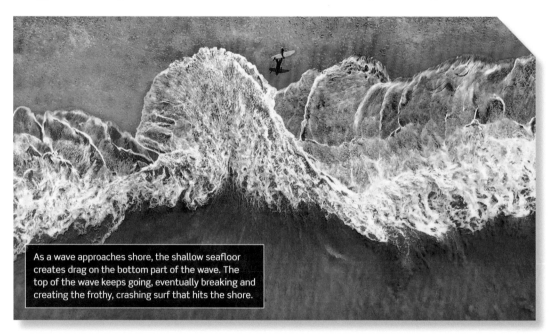

As a wave approaches shore, the shallow seafloor creates drag on the bottom part of the wave. The top of the wave keeps going, eventually breaking and creating the frothy, crashing surf that hits the shore.

A surfer rides a wave that's just starting to break. Waves are energy on the move.

Low tides expose some areas that are usually under-water. They're fun to explore!

capped, frothy ones that we see and hear crashing onshore at the beach. But if the wave does not hit land or a shallow bottom, its energy can keep traveling, sometimes across an entire ocean.

THE CHANGING TIDES

If you've been to the beach, you probably remember that sometimes you can walk far out from shore onto a soft sandbar, or find little tide pools filled with life. Later that same day, big waves crash on the shore at your feet. Where'd that sandbar go?

Tides—the regular rising and falling of ocean water—are responsible for this hide-and-seek game. Tides are out of this world. Really! The sun and the moon, and their gravity, make tides happen.

Gravity is the invisible force that pulls two objects toward each other. Because the moon is closer to Earth than the sun is, the moon's gravity has the greatest influence on the tides. As the moon orbits Earth, its gravity pulls the ocean toward it, making the ocean bulge on the side closest to the moon. A bulge also

it is felt as an up-and-down motion. But that little tug when the wave lets the board down is the water moving backward to complete its circular path.

As a wave reaches shallower water toward the shore, the seafloor creates drag on the bottom part, or trough, of the wave and slows the energy down. The crest of the wave continues to move forward at a faster pace than the trough. Soon, the wave tilts enough that it curls over, and it falls, or breaks. These breaking waves are the white-

Tide pools are small areas of water left onshore or between rocks when water has receded. This tide pool on the coast of Oregon, U.S.A., is filled with colorful sea stars and anemones.

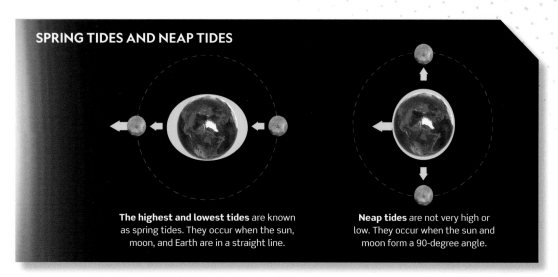

forms on the side of Earth farthest from the moon. How is that possible? It happens because of inertia, a force that keeps objects (or in this case, ocean water) moving in one direction. The moon is too far away for its gravity to overcome the inertia on this farthest side of the planet, and the water moves away from the Earth, forming a bulge.

As the moon circles Earth, Earth is also spinning on its axis, completing one full rotation in a day. So in 24 hours, every region of the planet passes through the two points where forces tug on the Earth (the gravitational-pull side and the inertia side) and create high tides. In the two points where those forces aren't acting on Earth, it's low tide. That's why most places on Earth experience two high and two low tides each day.

While the moon has the greatest effect on tides, the sun has an impact too. Like the moon, the sun's gravity pulls on Earth and the ocean. When the sun and moon are both pulling on the same side of Earth, the tides are larger than normal. These are called spring tides, and they occur twice a month all year long. (Their name is confusing: Spring tides happen in every season; the name refers to how the tide "springs forth.") When the sun

and moon are at right angles to each other, they pull in opposite directions, which partially cancels out the effects of their gravitational pull. This makes for smaller tides called neap tides.

While the forces acting on the ocean from the sun and the moon are constant, tidal range (the height difference between high and low tide) and tidal frequency (how often

THE POWERFUL FLOW OF TIDES IN AND OUT OF THE BAY OF FUNDY CAUSES THE OLD SOW WHIRLPOOL, WHICH MEASURES 250 FEET (75 M) WIDE. IT'S THE BIGGEST WHIRLPOOL IN THE WESTERN HEMISPHERE!

tides change) can vary. Geographical features can cause such variations. For example, the Bay of Fundy, off Canada's Atlantic coast, boasts the highest tides in the world. Twice each day, the tides push 176 billion tons (160 billion t) of water in and out of the bay. The bay's unique shape makes this possible. Because the mouth of the bay is much wider than where the water rushes into land, the bay acts as a funnel. That means that in the six hours it takes the tide to come in, the water piles up until it reaches a height of up to 50 feet (16 m) in some places at certain times of year. That's the size of a five-story

Boracay, Philippines, suffered heavy damage during super typhoon Haiyan in 2013.

building! In contrast, areas with long, flat coastlines often experience small differences between low and high tides, because the water flows over a much larger surface area.

SUPERSIZE STORMS

Tides, currents, and waves get ocean water moving, but nothing churns it up like the power of supersize storms and gigantic waves. In the Atlantic Ocean and the northeast Pacific, huge ocean storms are called hurricanes. They're known as typhoons in the North Pacific Ocean, and cyclones in the South Pacific or the Indian Ocean, but just remember that hurricanes, cyclones, and typhoons are the same. Some of these giant storms can grow to span an area bigger than the state of Texas!

No matter the name, the storms start the same way. They begin as small areas of rough weather called tropical atmospheric waves. These aren't water waves, but movements of air. Normally, tropical waves just cause heavy rains or strong winds. This happens because tropical waves create low-pressure areas. Air gets heated up over warm ocean waters, and that warm, wet air

rises, forming storm clouds. The area below that rising air has less pressure, and more air rushes in to fill the space, or vacuum, creating spinning winds. If a tropical wave begins swirling around the low-pressure area, the storm intensifies and becomes a tropical depression, which is a storm with winds of less than 39 miles an hour (62 km/h).

Strong, high-altitude winds from air currents called jet streams can barrel into a storm and break up its rotation before it grows bigger. But if enough warm water and moisture join a tropical depression, its winds

Hurricane Sandy, which hit the northeastern United States in 2012, had a supersize storm surge, flooding coastal areas.

may speed up: When winds are between 39 and 73 miles an hour (62 to 118 km/h), a tropical storm forms. When sustained wind speed reaches 74 miles an hour (119 km/h), a hurricane, cyclone, or typhoon forms. Meteorologists around the world name these storms and track them across the oceans to see if people need to prepare for the coming storm or even evacuate the area where they live.

When a hurricane-strength storm forms out at sea, it pulls water up underneath it, elevating the sea's surface. Strong winds from the storm also create big waves. As the storm moves toward land, both the elevated water and the strong waves get more power- ful and form a storm surge. The powerful storm surge rushes onshore, combining with the rain from the storm, sometimes flooding the coast—with the potential to damage hab- itats in and out of the water by wrecking reefs, damaging buildings, and flooding cities.

TSUNAMIS

Supersize storms are not the only events that rock the ocean. Underwater, large-scale geo- logic events, such as volcanic eruptions, land- slides, or earthquakes, can do the same. The energy from one of these events can sud-

THE SURGE OF WATER CREATED BY A TSUNAMI CAN MEASURE MORE THAN 100 FEET (30 M) HIGH!

denly displace a large mass of water in the ocean, creating a series of water waves called a tsunami.

In the deep ocean, it's hard to tell the size of the waves that these dramatic movements of the Earth's surface produce because of the long distances between waves and the depth of the ocean. Also, out at sea, tsu- namis can move at up to 500 miles an hour (805 km/h)—as fast as a jet airliner. But as these waves approach the shallower waters

TRY THIS
Creating a Low-Pressure System

1. Fill the empty glass with water, stopping about an inch from the rim at the top.

2. Place the poster board over the mouth of the glass.

3. Hold the glass in one hand, over the sink.

4. Gently place your other hand over the poster board and, while holding the board to the rim of the glass, slowly turn the glass upside down.

5. Slowly remove your hand from the poster board. The board should hold fast, keeping the water from spilling out.

Materials:
- Tall drinking glass
- Water
- Thick sheet of poster board, cut just wide enough to cover the mouth of the glass
- Large container or sink

What You Learned
This experiment demonstrates how areas of low pressure in the atmosphere create a vacuum. Because there is a small amount of air at the top of the glass when it is turned upside down, a vacuum is created. That air has a lower pressure than the water in the glass. This low-pressure air pulls the water in the glass upward and prevents the water from pushing the poster board down. The air pressure holds the poster board tight against the glass.

toward shore, they slow down and begin to bunch up, sometimes creating enormous walls of incoming water that flood streets, houses, and even towns along nearby shorelines.

When a tsunami nears the shore, the trough of a wave can sometimes get there first. It produces a vacuum effect, sucking water from the coastline rapidly toward the ocean. Seafloors—and sea life—are exposed. Boats can be left high and dry in harbors. This suctioning of the water is brief, but it is an important warning sign of a tsunami. Typically, about five minutes after the water has receded, a gigantic wave will crest and hit the shore. Sometimes, though, the crest of a wave will come first. But because a tsunami is not a single wave but rather a series of waves called a wave train, the first wave is not necessarily the most destructive. A tsunami wave train may come as a series of surges that are 10 minutes to two hours apart.

In 2011 a powerful magnitude 9 earthquake off of Japan produced a tsunami with waves 33 feet (10 m) high. Vehicles were swept away, buildings collapsed, and nearly 19,000 people were killed.

Since these catastrophic tsunamis, massive reconstruction and recovery efforts have helped rebuild schools, homes, and businesses. Because both Indonesia and Japan lie along the Ring of Fire (see p. 35), a horseshoe-shaped area along the rim of the Pacific Ocean where many of the world's earthquakes and volcanic eruptions occur, communities have developed better disaster management and preparedness plans. Scientists are also working to improve technology that can warn people living in coastal cities of incoming tsunamis.

ROGUE WAVES

While an undersea earthquake or rapidly rising or falling coastal waters could be a warning that a tsunami is coming, other powerful waves can appear with no warning at all. Mariners have long told of encounters with huge waves in the open ocean that seem to come out of nowhere.

For years, scientists thought claims of large open-ocean waves were just tall tales and did not take them seriously. But recent GPS satellites have recorded giant walls of

Tsunamis are caused by an underwater earthquake. Energy radiates out from the site and transfers to the water. This may cause large waves.

water, now called rogue waves, that lend truth to these stories. These single, unpredictable waves, which happen far out at sea, are at least twice the height of any other wave around them. Rogue waves have damaged and sunk even very large ships, and some believe they may be partly responsible for the sudden and mysterious disappearance of vessels from locations worldwide, like the Bermuda Triangle.

Scientists are still trying to determine how these colossal waves form. Some think they are created when ocean waves traveling in different directions and at different speeds "line up" for a few minutes, causing the water and energy of multiple waves to combine into one larger wave. Because rogue waves frequently occur in areas with strong ocean currents, others think they form when hurricane-force winds create waves that smack directly into a strong current—such as the Gulf Stream or the Agulhas Current—that is moving in the opposite direction. In this case, when these already tall waves run into a strong current, the collision produces one large, random wave. In 1995 a laser-based wave-height detector attached to the Draupner oil rig in the North Sea was recording 39-foot (12-m) waves during a storm. Suddenly, the same device measured a wave that was 85 feet (26 m) high. This was the first scientifically recorded proof of these rogue waves, a maritime myth no more.

COLOSSAL WAVES

Rogue waves pack some power. Here are some of the wildest waves that ships have encountered out at sea.

In 2005 a 70-foot (21-m) rogue wave hit the *Norwegian Dawn* cruise ship on a return trip from the Bahamas. The wave, which reached seven stories high, knocked out windows and flooded cabins.

In 1942 a rogue wave at least 75 feet (23 m) high, described as a "wall of water," smashed into the *Queen Mary* while the ship was carrying 16,683 American troops from New York to the United Kingdom. The ship tipped over into the water at an angle of 52 degrees and then righted itself. It would have turned over completely if it had leaned just three degrees more!

A 60-foot (18-m) rogue wave hits the *Overseas Chicago* tanker as it was headed south from Valdez, Alaska, in 1993.

In 1933 sailors on the navy tanker U.S.S. *Ramapo* measured an estimated 112-foot (34-m) rogue wave during a storm in the Pacific Ocean that had been blowing 69-to-76-mile-an-hour (111-to-122-km/h) gale force winds for days.

chapter 3

UNDERNEATH THE SURFACE

UNDERNEATH THE SURFACE

That globe sitting in your classroom once looked quite different than it does today. Millions of years ago, Earth's seven continents, or landmasses, were one massive supercontinent called Pangaea (meaning "all land"), which was surrounded by a single ocean called Panthalassa (meaning "all sea"). Over millions of years, through an aptly named process called continental drift, the continents slowly traveled, or drifted, into the configuration that you recognize today.

PLATE TECTONICS

How does this rearrangement of Earth's surface happen? Earth's crust—the solid-rock layer that is the ground we live on—is broken up into giant pieces called tectonic plates. They slide atop the Earth's mantle, the mostly solid middle section of our planet's interior.

These plates can move in one of three ways: sideways past each other, apart from one another, or into one another. Their movement is responsible for many landforms—such as mountains, valleys, volcanoes, and islands—that we see on land and in the ocean. Let's take a look at what the different kinds of motion create.

Usually, we don't feel the plates moving in any direction. But when plates slide sideways past each other, they don't slide smoothly. They grind against each other along fault lines, which are fractures, or breaks, in Earth's

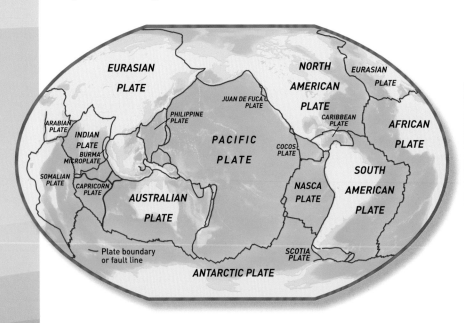

EURASIAN PLATE

NORTH AMERICAN PLATE

EURASIAN PLATE

JUAN DE FUCA PLATE

PHILIPPINE PLATE

ARABIAN PLATE

INDIAN PLATE

BURMA MICROPLATE

CARIBBEAN PLATE

AFRICAN PLATE

PACIFIC PLATE

COCOS PLATE

SOUTH AMERICAN PLATE

SOMALIAN PLATE

CAPRICORN PLATE

AUSTRALIAN PLATE

NASCA PLATE

— Plate boundary or fault line

SCOTIA PLATE

ANTARCTIC PLATE

Earth's surface is broken into pieces called tectonic plates, shown here. Some of those plates, such as the Pacific Plate, are covered by water.

Devastation in San Francisco, California, after the 1906 earthquake, which was magnitude 7.9

crust. When the pressure from the plates' movement is greater than the strength of the crust to hold together, the plates slip. This sudden movement causes an earthquake. The San Andreas Fault in California, U.S.A., is one of Earth's most active faults. It is more than 800 miles (1,300 km) long and at least 10 miles (16 km) deep. Movement of the plates along the fault triggered the 1906 San Francisco earthquake, which destroyed almost 500 city blocks, killing about 3,000 people. However, earthquakes aren't always destructive. They vary in their magnitude—which measures how much energy the plates release—and their intensity, or the strength of the shaking. Geologists estimate that we don't even feel 80 percent of the earthquakes that occur in a year.

When plates diverge, or move apart, in the deep ocean, a gap in the ocean floor forms. Magma, or melted rock, from deep in Earth's mantle rises up to fill the space between the plates. The magma cools and then hardens, forming a raised ridge called a mid-ocean ridge. The magma also spreads outward to form new seafloor, a process known as seafloor spreading. This cycle repeats endlessly, and the results of such repetition can be seen in the mid-ocean ridge system, a mountain chain—the world's longest—that loops through all the oceans. The mid-ocean ridge system is also the world's longest chain of volcanic mountains.

On land, when plates move apart, a valley-like rift—a crack in Earth's surface that widens over time—develops. The East African Rift, for example, runs 4,000 miles (6,400 km) through Ethiopia, Kenya, Uganda, and Malawi. Some of the world's deepest rift valleys are underwater. In the Mid-Atlantic Ridge, some of those valleys are as wide as nine miles (15 km).

The San Andreas Fault in California, one of Earth's most active faults

The Andes were formed when the Nasca tectonic plate slid beneath the South American plate as the plates collided.

What happens when plates collide? Oceanic crust (found under—you guessed it—the ocean) is denser than continental crust (found under a landmass), and when the two meet, the denser oceanic plate sinks beneath the lighter continental plate. This sinking is called subduction. As the oceanic plate slides into the Earth, it melts the continental plate above it. The resulting magma rises up through the crust, hardening to form volcanic mountain ranges near the coast of a continent, such as the Andes in South America. Sometimes, two continental plates collide without subducting, because both are too light to sink. In this case, the collision crunches and folds the rock along the boundary, lifting the rock up to form mountain ranges such as the Himalaya.

When two oceanic plates collide, however, the younger plate is less dense and rises, pushed up over the older, denser plate. The older plate sinks into the mantle and melts from the heat there. Magma rises

Marie Tharp

In the 1950s scientists at Columbia University in New York City used sonar to map the ocean's depth: An electronic signal was sent toward the seafloor, and a device noted how long it took for a microphone to record the signal's echo.

Women were not allowed on naval ships, so from her office desk, Marie Tharp interpreted her colleagues' data—from a 5,000-foot (1,524-m)-long roll of sonar readings—and created detailed, hand-drawn maps of the ocean floor.

At the time, scientists thought the ocean floor was flat, and meteorologist Alfred Wegener's theory of continental drift—that Earth's continents had once fit together but had drifted apart over millions of years—was dismissed, even mocked, among scientists.

As Tharp plotted the measurements, she saw that a V-shaped gap ran the length of a mountain range in the Atlantic Ocean (what would become known as the Mid-Atlantic Ridge). She concluded that this gap, a rift valley created by landmasses pulling apart, was evidence of continental drift.

Tharp had discovered the biggest geological feature on Earth—the mid-ocean ridge system—and had found proof of continental drift and seafloor spreading, key components of plate tectonics.

and erupts, forming a long, curved chain of volcanoes called an island arc. Indonesia and the Philippines were both formed this way. So if you live on or visit an island, your beach umbrella and chair might actually be sitting on the peak of a volcano that formed because one plate sank under another!

RING OF FIRE

Along the outer rim of the Pacific Ocean is a place where the collision of tectonic plates creates an area of high volcanic activity known as the Ring of Fire. A string of 452 volcanoes (both active and dormant) stretches from the southern tip of South America, up past the west coast of North America, across the Bering Strait, down along Japan, and into New Zealand, and reaches into the Indian Ocean. The Ring of Fire is home to two-thirds of all active volcanoes on Earth.

Several major volcanic events have happened along its expanse. In 1815 a volcano shook the area around Indonesia with what experts estimate was the most destructive explosion on Earth in the last 10,000 years. The volcano, called Mount Tambora, in Indonesia, blew 12 cubic miles (50 cubic km) of rock, dust, and gases up into the atmosphere and instantly killed about 10,000 people on the island of Sumbawa.

The eruption of Mount St. Helens, a volcano in Washington State, U.S.A., created the largest landslide in recorded history. In 1980 this explosion took 1,300 feet (396 m) off the top of the volcano, flattening forests and generating dangerous mudflows. Fifty-seven people died because of the blast, which scattered ash across 12 states.

About 90 percent of Earth's earthquakes also occur along the Ring of Fire. Both of the deadliest tsunamis of the 21st century (Indonesia in 2004 and Japan in 2011) were triggered by powerful earthquakes that originated in the Ring of Fire.

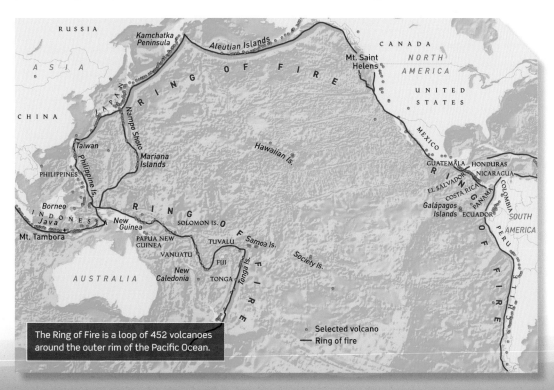

The Ring of Fire is a loop of 452 volcanoes around the outer rim of the Pacific Ocean.

SEAMOUNTS

Seamounts, underwater mountains formed by volcanic activity, appear as isolated peaks or as part of a larger chain. Many are extinct volcanoes, standing quiet on the ocean floor. (Unlike in the animal kingdom where "extinct" means an animal no longer exists, an extinct volcano means it no longer erupts.) Seamounts are found throughout the world's oceans, but many appear in the Pacific because of the higher rate of volcanic activity that occurs there. They rise at least 3,280 feet (1,000 m) above the surrounding seafloor. Some tower as high as 13,000 feet (3,962 m), but the tops of seamounts are often still hundreds or even thousands of feet below the water's surface.

Seamounts are an oasis for a variety of ocean life. Deep-moving currents run into these hulking undersea landforms and force

SHARK VOLCANO

In 2015 National Geographic Explorer Dr. Brennan Phillips headed to Kavachi Volcano, a seamount in the Solomon Islands in the South Pacific Ocean that is one of the most active underwater volcanoes on Earth. It erupted more than two dozen times in the 20th century, and again in 2004, 2007, and 2014. Because the water around the volcano is extremely hot and acidic, Dr. Phillips and his team sent camera-equipped robots to explore Kavachi. Some of the footage is pictured here. The cameras caught the expected—carbon dioxide and methane gas bubbles rising from seafloor vents—and the unexpected: silky sharks and hammerhead sharks swimming around in the top of the volcano! The team didn't expect anything but bacteria to inhabit the waters around Kavachi, so the presence of these sharks in the volcano, as well as crabs, jellyfish, and stingrays, was quite a surprise.

Scientists don't know how the sharks handle Kavachi's high heat and acid. And their presence raises another question: Can the sharks sense an eruption coming? If so, and if scientists can figure out how they sense it, the answer could help them figure out how to keep people living near the Ring of Fire, where active volcanoes can be a threat, safer.

water upward. This water carries up nutrients from dead plants and animals from the depths—a perfect snack for the corals, sponges, and sea anemones that cluster on some seamounts' rocky slopes. Crabs and brittle stars join the feast, and small lobsters and fish burrow in the coral. At some seamounts, larger ocean animals, like tuna and humpback whales, stop to feed on the number of small fish that thrive there, and scalloped hammerhead sharks find mates.

The coastline of Oahu, Hawaii, is dotted with volcanic hot spots.

HOT SPOTS

Some volcanoes form right in the middle of tectonic plates, instead of at the edges of the plates as they do in the mid-ocean ridge system. These volcanoes are created by hot spots, weaker areas of the Earth's crust where magma from Earth's mantle pushes up to the surface.

This is how the Hawaiian Islands formed. The islands are volcanoes that were created by magma erupting over a long period of time. The cooling magma piled up, forming an island. Then, over millions of years, as the tectonic

plate moved past the hot spot, new volcanoes formed. Seamounts now underwater to the northwest of Hawaii are the oldest mountains in this chain. The youngest mountains include all the Hawaiian Islands, which are above the water's surface. That includes the Big Island of Hawaii, which has active volcanoes, and a new volcano, Loihi, that is forming underwater to the southeast. Someday, Loihi will become another Hawaiian island for people to visit!

TRY THIS

Make Your Own Hot-Spot Volcano

Materials:
- Window screen
- Foam shaving cream in aerosol can

1. With a partner, hold each end of a window screen horizontally so that the screen is between you.

2. Find a third person to help you hold the can of shaving cream beneath one end of the screen.

3. Holding the screen, you and your partner slowly slide the screen past the third person.

4. The third person sprays the shaving cream up through the screen in occasional bursts as the screen slides by.

What You Learned
The screen serves as a tectonic plate. The slow movement of the screen, or tectonic plate, over the stationary hot spot (the can of shaving cream) will eventually create a trail of volcanoes (the balls of shaving cream) on land (the screen). The oldest volcanoes are the ones farthest from the hot spot.

TIDAL AND OCEAN ZONES

1 HELLO, THERE! I'M CAPTAIN AQUATICA. I NOTICED YOU FROM THE WATER BELOW, AND I JUST WANTED TO SEE IF YOU NEEDED A HAND. ER ... TENTACLE? ANYWAY, YOU SEEM LOST.

2 LOST? NO! I—THE MIGHTY AND TERRIBLE CRIMSON CALAMITY—COULD NEVER BE LOST! I AM THE PACIFIC OCEAN'S MOST INFAMOUS TENTACLED TERROR!

SEA URCHINS SHIVER AT THE MERE THOUGHT OF ME. ATOP THIS HIGH LEDGE, I STRIKE FEAR INTO THE HEARTS OF MARINE LIFE FROM HERE TO THE HORIZON.

3 I SEE. I DON'T MEAN TO QUESTION YOUR ... AUTHORITY. BUT IT SEEMS TO ME THAT YOU MIGHT BE MORE COMFORTABLE IN THE WATER ... OR IN THE LOW INTERTIDAL ZONE, AT THE VERY LEAST.

TIDAL AND OCEAN ZONES

The part of a beach that is above water at low tide and below water at high tide is called the intertidal zone. It is divided into four parts: the splash zone, the upper intertidal zone, the middle intertidal zone, and the low intertidal zone. Each of these areas has a unique ecosystem—a community of living things and their habitat, or where they live.

ANIMALS IN DIFFERENT TIDAL AND OCEAN ZONES HAVE UNIQUE ADAPTATIONS THAT ALLOW THEM TO THRIVE DEPENDING ON FACTORS LIKE WATER, SUNLIGHT, AND TEMPERATURE.

THE SPLASH ZONE

The splash zone might sound like something you'd find at a waterpark, but it is the intertidal zone farthest from the sea. Seawater

Acorn barnacles feeding

almost never covers the splash zone. At high tide, breaking waves crash against rocks and sand, spraying mist onto this zone. Even this small amount of water keeps the area soggy. Most of the time, the sun beats down on the splash zone, which can dry it out. For this reason, plants have a hard time growing here, and few animals can survive.

One exception is the buckshot barnacle. A barnacle is a type of arthropod, an animal that has jointed feet, a segmented body, and an exoskeleton, or a skeleton that is outside its body. Barnacles attach themselves to the rocks in the splash zone and live together in large clusters. At first glance, they may look more like empty shells than living creatures. But when sea spray wets the splash zone, they stretch their delicate, feathery limbs into the mist. Their limbs filter out microscopic plants and animals called plankton. The barnacles then quickly pull their limbs back in and eat their catch.

The common periwinkle snail, a type of mollusk, lives here too. Mollusks are a group of invertebrates—animals without a backbone—that have soft, unsegmented bodies, live in damp areas, and usually have a protective shell. At high tide, the common periwinkle drags its shell over rocky surfaces, searching for small patches of algae called sea lettuce to nibble on. As the tide recedes and the sun dries out the splash zone, barnacles and snails tuck into their shells to stay moist until high tide returns.

Waves hit the splash zone in Cozumel, Mexico.

UPPER INTERTIDAL ZONE

Closer to the sea is the upper intertidal zone. On the California coastline, for example, strong ocean waves batter the rocky upper intertidal zone during high tide. Many animals that live here have hard shells that help shield them from the rough waves. One example is a chiton. Like the common periwinkle, the chiton is also a type of mollusk. With its oval-shaped shell, the chiton looks like it is wearing a suit of armor, with overlapping plates that protect it. This creature slides its single foot over the rocks, feeling for algae and scraping it off with its rough tongue.

Limpets are a type of snail with hard, dome-shaped shells. Like chitons, they eat algae. But they graze only during high tide. During low tide, the upper intertidal zone is too dry. To keep from drying up, limpets use the edge of their shell to carve out a shallow space in the rocks. They stick to the rock by suction, forming a little hollow of a home that fits them perfectly. But it doesn't keep limpets completely safe. Hungry crabs lurk nearby. Sometimes the crabs can wrench a limpet from its rocky hole and eat it. And sometimes, a seagull makes a meal of the crab!

MIDDLE INTERTIDAL ZONE

Farther down the beach toward the surf, in the middle intertidal zone, animals have adapted to survive in constantly changing and challenging conditions. When the area is underwater during high tides, they must avoid underwater

A sea star clings to an algae-covered rock in the middle intertidal zone.

TIDE POOLS

On a rocky shore during low tide, pockets of water get trapped among the rocks. These are tide pools, and they can range in size from puddles to small ponds. This one is located in Salt Point State Park, outside of San Francisco, California.

Tide pools are a great place to see colorful anemones, a relative of coral polyps and jellyfish, wave their pretty but venom-filled tentacles to catch fish swimming by. Sea stars suction themselves in clusters across the rocks. Crabs and their cousins, lobsters, walk along the bottom of the pool. An octopus could make an appearance too.

The animals found in tide pools have to be tough, though, because their home is constantly changing. The water level shifts as seawater flows in and out with the tides. When a big wave crashes in, tide pool animals and plants have to be able to hang on tight to avoid getting washed into the ocean. During low tide, or on a hot day when water evaporates (turns into vapor), some creatures are left more visible to hungry shorebirds. Some, like the decorator crab, which attaches tiny animals to its shell, use camouflage to hide from predators. Others use defenses to keep predators away. For example, sea urchins use their prickly spines to poke or poison predators. The blazing sun also affects the pool's temperature, its salinity (or saltiness), and oxygen levels. Animals such as the sculpin, a fish, can breathe air for a few hours when there is less water around. In this image, sea stars feed on mussels in a tide pool. An array of adaptations keep tide pool animals thriving in their unique environment.

Purple sea urchins dot the shallow water of a tide pool.

predators and protect themselves from powerful waves that could dislodge them. During low tides, they must be able to handle exposure to air and avoid land and air predators that can eat them, such as lizards, sea otters, seagulls, and pelicans. In this zone, hermit crabs crawl along the edge of the water. Just offshore might be a bed of mussels that have anchored themselves to the rocky reef. Predators like sea stars feed on mid-zone mussels. They grip a mussel with their strong suckered feet and pry open the shell. Then the sea star lowers its stomach into the opening and begins to digest the mussel. Soon all that is left is an empty shell.

LOW INTERTIDAL ZONE

The low intertidal zone is almost always underwater, except during a very low tide. Many organisms live here. Fish such as opaleyes lay their eggs in this zone. Once hatched, the young fish stay in the shallows until they are big enough to survive in kelp forests and rocky underwater areas. A kind of brown algae called sea palm, which sways back and forth in the current, thrives here.

Purple sea urchins feed on the sea palm. The urchins have sharp spines that offer protection from most predators, but certain cephalopods, members of the mollusk family that include squid and octopuses, have figured out a way around an urchin's armor. An East Pacific red octopus, for example, can reach out its arm and flip an urchin upside down— an easy way to suck out its soft insides.

OCEAN ZONES

Just as the shore and its shallow waters are divided into four tidal zones, each with its own unique characteristics and sea life, the ocean is also divided into zones, all included in the pelagic (open ocean) space. These five zones are based on depth and the amount of light that reaches each zone. They are also identifiable by the kinds of plants and animals found in each one. The deeper the water, the darker and colder it gets. Greater depth also brings greater pressure, due to the weight of water pressing down from above. Different animals inhabit different zones, many displaying unique adaptations that allow them to live in darker, colder waters.

A school of fish swim through rays of light in the sunlit zone.

THE SUNLIT ZONE

From microscopic algae called phytoplankton to jellyfish and giant whale sharks, the sunlit zone is thriving with life. Because sunlight reaches a depth of about 660 feet (200 m), phytoplankton, longer strands of algae called seaweed, and flowering marine plants like seagrass are able to grow. They use energy from the sun to make food, a process called photosynthesis. This sunlit zone is also a feeding ground and home for many of the ocean's animals, including sea turtles, stingrays, fish, dolphins, corals, and many other creatures.

THE TWILIGHT ZONE

Deeper down is the twilight zone. It ranges from about 660 to 3,250 feet (200 to 1,000 m) deep. This area of the ocean is dim and murky, and the water is cooler than in the sunlit zone. Little light reaches it, so plants cannot grow. Some of the animals that make the twilight zone their home are bioluminescent, meaning they can produce their own light. Highlight hatchetfish, for example, have organs called photophores on their undersides once they reach adulthood. These light-producing organs, which can change intensity to match the amount of light coming from above, help the fish blend in so they're not as visible to predators below. The northern stoplight loosejaw dragonfish is named for the photophores

The northern stoplight loosejaw dragonfish

The female deep sea anglerfish, with its glowing "fishing rod" organ

found under each eye—one is green and one is red—that use light to find food. These fish also use their "loose" jaws and needle-like teeth to capture prey. They also dive deeper than the twilight zone, in depths of up to a thousand feet (305 m). Other animals that live in the twilight zone, like the blobfish, simply float, waiting for food to swim by or drift down from above.

THE MIDNIGHT ZONE

The dark midnight zone ranges from 3,250 to 13,000 feet (1,000 to 4,000 m) deep. Sunlight does not reach this zone. The weight of all the water above leads to intense pressure, but many midnight-zone animals, like the Atolla jellyfish, are soft-bodied and able to withstand the tremendous pressure in the midnight zone.

Bioluminescent animals offer the only light found in the midnight zone. Food is scarce here, and these creatures use their flickering bodies to attract the next meal. The female Kroyer's deep sea anglerfish, for example, has

a dorsal spine tipped with a light-producing organ that resembles a fishing rod. The end of this lure is filled with glowing bacteria. When

THERE ARE MORE THAN 200 SPECIES OF ANGLERFISH. THOUGH MOST ARE SMALL, SOME CAN REACH LENGTHS OF MORE THAN THREE FEET (NEARLY 1 M).

the fish flashes its blue-green light, other fish come in for a closer look, hoping for an easy meal. That's when the lady anglerfish snaps her jaws shut and swallows the curious prey whole. (Male anglerfish do not have this same luminous protrusion, so they latch onto the females with their sharp teeth, riding along as passengers rather than hunting as predators themselves.)

There are bigger predators in this zone too. Sperm whales dive down to these depths to hunt for food that other creatures can't reach. The whales catch many types of squid.

Comb jellies are bioluminescent. They have proteins that go through a chemical reaction to produce either blue or green light. Scientists think this is a defensive mechanism.

BIOLUMINESCENCE AND BIOFLUORESCENCE

Bioluminescent animals can produce their own light, either with organs called photophores, like the hatchetfish does, or by hosting other organisms that give off light. An example is the anglerfish. Bacteria live in a lure attached to the fish's head. The bacteria give off light that helps the anglerfish catch prey. These animals would have a hard time existing in their pitch-black world without being able to create this "living light."

But even some creatures that live in the sunlit zone use light. Unlike bioluminescent animals that produce their own light, biofluorescent animals are able to absorb blue ocean light and transform it into different colors, usually as neon greens or reds. In the all-blue realm of the ocean, biofluorescence helps many creatures create color to find and communicate with each other. Their eyes are also sensitive to the colors transformed by biofluorescence, as it creates contrast in their all-blue environment.

For humans to best visualize these underwater light shows, special camera lenses are helpful. Scientists have long studied corals known to use biofluorescence, but they've only recently discovered that this phenomenon extends to over 200 fish species, including some eels, sharks, lizardfish, and even sea turtles such as this hawksbill.

Mussels, shrimp, and tube worms in the Gulf of Mexico, in the abyssal zone's hydrothermal vents

their way to animals like sea lilies and sea pens that filter it from the water. The tripod fish balances carefully on the seafloor, supported on its fins as it waits for a meal to drift by. Around hydrothermal vents—cracks in the seafloor that spew jets of hot water that can reach temperatures of over 700°F (370°C)—live giant tube worms and species of clams, crabs, and shrimp.

THE ABYSSAL ZONE

The abyssal zone begins at a depth of 13,000 feet (4,000 m) and descends to 19,700 feet (6,000 m). This even deeper, darker area of the ocean may not seem like it could support life, but some animals do call this zone home. Like many creatures in the midnight zone, those in the abyssal zone rely on food that trickles down from above. Called marine snow, these food particles make

THE HADAL ZONE

The hadal zone is found within the ocean's deepest trenches. It ranges from 19,700 to 36,000 feet (6,000 to 11,000 m) deep. But even at these extreme depths, life exists. Acorn worms sift through sediment to find whatever tiny morsels of food might have

SOME SCIENTISTS LOOK TO THE HADAL ZONE—AN EXTREME ENVIRONMENT—TO HELP THEM UNDERSTAND HOW LIFE COULD EXIST ON OTHER PLANETS.

fallen from above. And strange-looking pink sea cucumbers called sea pigs slurp up tiny organisms from the muddy seafloor.

A sea pig crawls along the seafloor in the hadal zone, the deepest part of the ocean.

chapter 5

ECOSYSTEM ENGINEERS

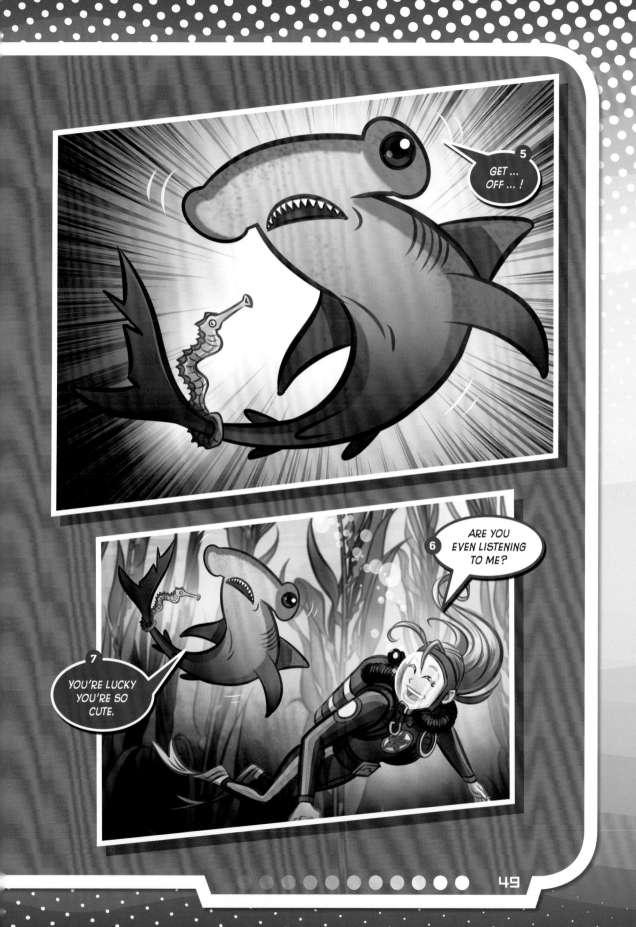

ECOSYSTEM ENGINEERS

O cean habitats are packed with sea life. Corals create reefs, which are like underwater cities that attract hundreds of ocean species with food and hiding spots. Seagrass and a type of algae called kelp grow into dense underwater forests. Some species of oysters pile together, building areas called beds—and other sea creatures move in too. In the ocean, certain animals and plants—like corals, kelp, seagrass, and oysters—create or modify habitats to such a degree that they are called ecosystem engineers. That is, they construct rich and unique living spaces for a variety of other plants and animals. Let's take a closer look at each of these ecosystem engineers and the habitats and communities they create.

COLORFUL CORAL REEFS

Coral reefs are found in tropical areas of the ocean where the water is warm and clear enough for sunlight to pass through it. Coral reefs are made up of many individual corals, which are home to algae that keep the corals healthy. Here's how hard or stony corals are formed: Baby coral larvae drift in the ocean until they attach themselves to a hard surface, like a rock or another coral. As the larvae grow into tiny tube-shaped animals called coral polyps, they build a hard outer skeleton made of calcium carbonate that helps to protect the soft coral polyp from predators. Some corals don't have the hard outer skeleton, though—these are called soft corals. Corals can attach to other corals, slowly building a reef over time.

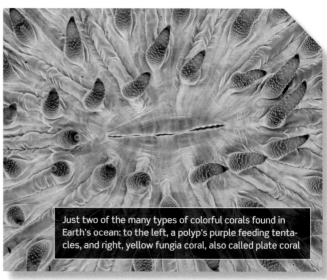

Just two of the many types of colorful corals found in Earth's ocean: to the left, a polyp's purple feeding tentacles, and right, yellow fungia coral, also called plate coral

A reef in the waters off Indonesia is busy with marine life.

Corals get the energy they need in several ways. Most hard corals have algae called zooxanthellae living within them. The algae use sunlight to produce sugar, and a lot of that sugar is absorbed by the polyp. They also rely on their inhabitants to process nutrients. Corals also eat bits of floating animal and plant waste, as well as live zooplankton (see p. 52), which they catch at night. They extend their long stinging tentacles and pull them back in to digest the prey that gets stuck to them.

Coral reefs cover less than one percent of our ocean, but they are home to 25 percent of marine life. Fish, sponges, sea slugs, shrimp, jellyfish, sea turtles, and eels are just some of the animals that call coral reefs home. Coral reefs are an important part of the ocean ecosystem. They provide permanent sources of shelter and food for many animals, including humans. Coral reefs also offer protection from storms for coastal communities and they are a source of recreation for us—many people travel the world to catch a glimpse of the sea life on coral reefs.

SCIENTIST PROFILE

Kakani Katija

Bioengineer Dr. Kakani Katija studies jellyfish movement. She tracks them over long distances with sensors. She also uses colored dyes to see how they move through water. She has found that they are important agents of seawater mixing and that they move nutrients around their environment. Her new research is on designing ROVs (see p. 98) that can follow jellies in the twilight zone.

BOTTOM OF THE FOOD WEB

Just as coral reefs are crucial to the ocean ecosystem, tiny organisms called plankton also play an important role in sustaining sea life. Out in the open ocean, living at or near the surface of the water, are two kinds of plankton. Phytoplankton are microscopic algae. "Phyto" means "plantlike" and "plankton" means "drifting," so while some phytoplankton use whiplike tails, or flagella, to move through the water, many simply float wherever the water takes them. Like land plants, they depend on sunlight to live and use the energy from sunlight to make food out of water and air by photosynthesis. When they get a lot of sunlight and nutrients, they bloom, making their microscopic selves visible by turning the water green.

Zooplankton, which are tiny animals, drift too. Some are microscopic, and others are small but can be seen with the naked eye. This zoo of floating animals includes the tiny eggs of crabs, lobsters, many species of fish, and sea stars, as well as marine worms, jellyfish, and shrimplike krill.

As the bottom, or base, of the ocean food web—or simply put, the system of who gets to eat who in the water—phytoplankton ultimately nourish every creature swimming in the sea. How is this possible? Zooplankton, small fish, and mussels eat phytoplankton. Then larger fish and other predators like sharks eat these smaller creatures. Plants and animals in the ocean are all connected, and the drifting, microscopic phytoplankton are vital to this web.

Life on the Great Barrier Reef: Here, a dugong roots for seagrass; top right, the Great Barrier reef from above; bottom right, a colorful threadfin butterflyfish.

THE GREAT BARRIER REEF

The Great Barrier Reef is the world's largest and most complex group of coral reefs. Located off the northeast coast of Australia, the reef stretches for 1,400 miles (2,300 km). That's as far as the distance between Maine and the middle of Arizona, U.S.A. This large ecosystem is vital to marine life. The 600 species of hard and soft corals found here support 1,625 species of fish (including sharks), 3,000 types of mollusk, plus other animals like crustaceans. More than 30 species of whales and dolphins swim in the waters surrounding the reefs, and six of the world's seven marine turtle species can be found swimming through.

The dugong, a marine mammal that looks a lot like the manatees that inhabit the coastline of Florida, U.S.A, can also be found along the reef. Both manatees and dugongs are related to elephants and have front flippers that they use for steering as they glide through the water. However, while manatees have paddle-like tails, dugongs have tails that are fluked, or V-shaped, like a whale's. This large but gentle animal can hold its breath for up to six minutes while it roots around for underwater seagrasses with its bristled, sensitive snout. Dugongs usually live alone or in pairs, but they are social animals that have been observed in groups of a hundred.

THE GREAT BARRIER REEF IS SO LARGE, YOU CAN SEE IT FROM SPACE! AND BECAUSE CORALS MAKE UP THE REEF, THEY'RE ONE OF THE FEW LIVING THINGS YOU CAN SEE FROM SPACE.

Fish flourish along the Great Barrier Reef. One common type found here are butterflyfish. Some have dark bands across their eyes and round dots on their tail that help disguise a butterflyfish's head from its tail when predators are nearby. The confusion that this creates can give the fish an extra second to

escape. The butterflyfish uses its small mouth to eat coral polyps or algae growing on the reef.

Where there are fish, there are also sharks. Many shark species live near reefs. Bottom-dwelling carpet sharks like the tasseled wob-begong camouflage themselves on the seafloor. A mass of skin that looks like a shaggy beard flaps around its jaws, helping this shark blend in. But the most common sharks on the Great Barrier Reef are whitetip reef sharks, blacktip reef sharks, and gray reef sharks. These are the species that people most frequently encounter while snorkel-ing or diving.

Tiger sharks, which also often inhabit coral reefs, get their name from the striped pattern found on young or juvenile sharks. The pat-tern may fade with age as these sharks grow to become top predators. As adults, they can grow up to 18 feet (5 m) long. Tiger sharks'

powerful jaws are lined with serrated teeth that can crack open sea turtle shells. These sharks patrol the local waters and will eat almost anything. In addition to their conventional meals of seals, seabirds, stingrays, and sea snakes, old tires and car license plates have also been found in the stomachs of tiger sharks!

Fourteen species of sea snakes can be found within the Great Barrier Reef. With their long, thin bodies, these venomous snakes, such as the olive sea snake and the black-and-white banded sea krait, wriggle in and out of small crevices between corals to look for prey. Their paddle-like tail helps them move through the water. And their lungs extend nearly the full length of their body—plus they can extract oxygen from the water through their skin. This allows sea snakes to stay on the seafloor for up to two hours before they need to return to the surface for air.

A diver explores a kelp forest.

KELP FORESTS

Kelp forests are formed by large species of brown algae that thrive in cool and shallow coastal waters around the world. Some kelp species, like giant kelp, can grow up to two feet (61 cm) per day. There are several species of kelp that are large enough to create underwater forests. They all anchor themselves to rocky areas or the seafloor using a rootlike structure called a holdfast. And they all have leafy blades that stick out to collect sunlight, like leaves on land plants do. Some species, such as bull kelp and giant kelp that grow off the California coast, are near enough to each other to form massive kelp forests, also known as kelp beds.

Just like trees in land-based forests, kelp species in underwater forests use sunlight energy to grow, remove carbon dioxide from the atmosphere, and help create the oxygen we need to breathe.

SCIENTIST PROFILE

Vinay Udyawer

Studying venomous sea snakes sounds like a dangerous job. But Dr. Vinay Udyawer is determined to find out the impact human activities such as fishing are having on the health of the Great Barrier Reef's resident serpents. The numbers of some species of sea snake are declining, while other species' populations remain steady. Dr. Udyawar wants to know why that is, and how some species are surviving better than others. To do this, he tags sea snakes and monitors their movements. This information can help him understand what habitats are important for sea snakes and how far they move to find them.

Dr. Udyawer recently found an important nursery habitat for sea snakes in Australia's Cleveland Bay. There, he located many pregnant and juvenile sea snakes belonging to two species: spine-bellied sea snakes and elegant sea snakes. Giving birth to young in shallower, protected waters such as this bay may give sea snakes a better chance to survive. They will become adults before having to face larger predators and fishing nets in deeper waters offshore. Identifying and protecting important habitats like this can give these unique serpents a chance to survive the immense pressures they face from fishing, coastal development, and climate change.

MANGROVE FORESTS

Like reef-building corals, mangrove forests are ecosystem engineers. These trees grow in tropical and subtropical areas along ocean coastlines and in the mudflats of estuaries, where freshwater from rivers and streams mixes with the ocean's salt water in bays, harbors, or inlets.

These trees survive because of a few key adaptations. Their curved roots are like stilts that hold the trees above the incoming tide. When the tide is low, the roots absorb oxygen. Mangroves also filter out as much as 90 percent of the salt from the seawater that enters their roots. Some trees get rid of the salt through glands in their leaves. Others concentrate the salt in older bark or leaves, which drop off. Mangrove trees also store water in thick leaves that protect against evaporation.

Mangroves provide shelter and nutrients for a range of wildlife. Where three rivers converge at the ocean along the border of India and Bangladesh is the world's largest mangrove ecosystem. This waterlogged forest, called the Sundarbans, is home to spotted deer, snakes, and Bengal tigers. Dolphins, including the Ganges dolphins and Irrawaddy dolphins, swim the waterways. In the United States, the mangroves off Florida's southern coast house worms, horseshoe crabs, and even alligators among their roots. Mangroves also line coastal areas of Thailand, pictured here. Hundreds of species of seabirds inhabit Thailand's mangrove forests.

A sea otter floats in kelp off the coast of California.

Fish gather in kelp forests for food and shelter. In Southern California and Northern Baja California, Mexico, brightly colored garibaldi fish and giant sea bass are often found in these pillars of seaweed. Kelp forests are nurseries for many young animals, such as rockfish, who hide from predators in kelp stands until they are grown and better able to protect themselves. Even gray whales seek safety in kelp forests. Females with offspring often swim through the forests to avoid orcas that target their young. Harbor seals also frequent these leafy underwater forests, searching for an easy meal.

Sea otters thrive in kelp forests too. These marine mammals play an important role in keeping these unique habitats healthy. Otters eat a lot—about a quarter of their weight every day, which means they can eat about 15 pounds (7 kg) of food a day! They feed on mollusks and crustaceans, as well as sea urchins—small, spiny creatures that eat kelp. By eating sea urchins, otters keep the urchin population from growing too large. If the

MMM, THAT'S GOOD KELP! PEOPLE CAN EAT KELP TOO. IT'S RICH IN IRON, CALCIUM, AND VITAMIN K. KOMBU, A TYPE OF KELP, IS USED TO MAKE DASHI, A DELICIOUS BROTH USED IN JAPANESE COOKING.

otters weren't there, the urchins could form large herds and move along the ocean floor, eating the holdfasts that keep the kelp in place. The kelp would float away and kelp forests would be destroyed. Because otters prevent this from happening, they are considered a keystone species, which are species that a habitat depends on for survival.

KELP NEED HELP

Kelp forests that grow off the coast of Tasmania, a large island south of Australia, are in trouble. Over the last 80 years, Tasmania has lost 95 percent of the kelp forests off its eastern coast, due in part to climate change, as well as a current that affected the water temperatures. In the past two decades, winter water temperatures have risen by 3°F (1.7°C), making it hard for the kelp to grow back after seasonal storms. But the warmer water has also contributed to a second threat. Sea urchins thrive in warmer waters, so their populations in the area have grown. Urchins eat the holdfasts that keep the kelp attached to the seafloor, which threatens the kelp's survival. Normally, there aren't enough urchins to do serious damage. But the urchins' natural predator in this area, rock lobsters, have been overfished. With so few predators around to eat them, the urchins multiply—and chomp away at the kelp holdfasts.

SEAGRASS MEADOWS

Seagrass is often confused with seaweed. However, seagrass is more closely related to the flowering plants found on land, as these plants have roots, stems, and leaves, and they produce flowers and seeds. Seagrasses can form dense underwater meadows in shallow saltwater habitats, making them one of the most productive ecosystems in the world: 10 square feet (1 sq m) of seagrass can generate 2.6 gallons (10 L) of oxygen every day by using the energy from sunlight. Many of these plants are a few feet tall. But the tallest species—an eelgrass called *Zostera caulescens* that grows off the coast of Japan and other northeast Asian countries, can reach 23 feet (7 m) high.

Smaller organisms such as shrimp, some fish species, algae, sponges, and

> MOST OF THE OXYGEN IN EARTH'S ATMOSPHERE IS GENERATED BY MARINE PLANTS, WHICH INCLUDE PHYTOPLANKTON, SEAWEEDS, AND SEAGRASSES.

Birds called oystercatchers scour an oyster reef off the coast of Texas for food.

sea anemones live on and between blades of seagrass. That abundant life attracts animals such as larger fish, octopuses, and sharks that eat the smaller animals. And green sea turtles and manatees graze on the seagrass itself. Seagrass meadows are home to about 40,000 fish species and millions of invertebrates. Like coral reefs and mangrove forests, they also serve as nurseries for juvenile marine species and provide protection from predators and rough ocean waters. Some seagrass meadows have been around for thousands of years, and many can even be seen from space, such as those in the Red Sea off the coast of Saudi Arabia.

OYSTER REEFS

Some oyster species, including the eastern oyster, cluster on top of one another. Over time, as new oysters pile on top, this group of ecosystem engineers creates small reefs near shorelines and in estuaries of the southern United States. Oyster reefs make a great home for smaller marine animals. Mollusks such as clams, mussels, and conchs can nestle into these reefs, as well as many types of worms. Fish such as gobies, snappers, and sea trout hide and hunt for food here. Oyster reefs are also crawling with crustaceans such as mud crabs, green crabs, and blue crabs, all searching for barnacles, other crabs, and dead fish to forage on.

OCEAN ANIMALS

OCEAN ANIMALS

The ocean makes up 70 percent of Earth's surface. These vast waters are home to many thousands of species. Those species include many mammals, fish, and birds—and many, many more invertebrates. Scientists say we've explored only about 20 percent of the ocean, which means that there's still 80 percent to explore and map. New species are still being discovered. Let's take a look at a few of the ocean's many amazing animals.

MAGNIFICENT MARINE MAMMALS

What makes an animal a mammal? All mammals breathe air, grow hair, are warm-blooded, and most have live babies (monotremes are the only mammals that lay eggs). Mammal moms also nurse their babies. Marine mammals are mammals that do all that *and* have adapted to depend on the ocean for their food and survival.

Marine mammals include whales and dolphins (they have a bit of hair) and even polar bears and sea otters. Let's meet some magnificent marine mammals.

HUMPBACK WHALE

Humpback whales live in ocean waters all over the world. But in the North Pacific, some of these whales make seasonal migrations that are one of the longest mammal migrations on Earth. Over the summer, they feed heavily in the waters off of Alaska, loading up on krill, plankton, and many small species of fish. When fall arrives, they leave these frigid waters and begin a steady, nearly nonstop swim to winter breeding grounds off the coast of Hawaii. The journey takes six to eight weeks and covers 6,000 miles (9,700 km). But the whales don't all get there at the same time.

The first to arrive are mother whales still nursing calves that are about a year old.

A humpback whale mother rubs against her calf.

They show up between the middle and end of November. Next, other juvenile whales that are no longer nursing arrive, followed by the adult males. After that come other adult females. The last whales to show up are pregnant females. Pregnant humpback whales stay in Alaskan waters longer than all other humpbacks so they can eat as much as possible and gain weight before their migration journey. They will need the extra weight and energy to be able to feed their hungry calves.

SHORT-BEAKED COMMON DOLPHIN

You might be more familiar with the bottlenose dolphin, but the short-beaked common dolphin is actually one of the most plentiful dolphin species in the ocean. These dolphins are on the smaller side—most measure about 6 feet (2 m) and weigh about 170 pounds (77 kg). But they are remarkable for their patterning: known as an hourglass pattern, they have what looks like a cape of dark gray or black running down their backs, which plunges downward at their dorsal fin. Below the line of gray-black is patterning of tan or yellow, light gray, and white.

Short-beaked common dolphins live in oceans worldwide, but they especially like rocky undersea areas, like seamounts and ridges, and

A short-beaked common dolphin surfaces in the Atlantic Ocean.

Asha de Vos

Asha de Vos is a whale biologist who discovered a population of blue whales that live year-round in the waters off her island home of Sri Lanka, in the Indian Ocean. Before this discovery, it was believed that all large whales migrated between cold water feeding areas and warm water mating and birthing areas. The blue whales Dr. de Vos discovered do not migrate. They not only breed and have babies in these warm tropical waters, but they also feed here, making them quite unique. Why do they stay in one area? Because Sri Lanka's monsoonal climate drives ocean circulation in such a way that this area is more food rich than you would expect. This in turn ensures a steady supply of food for the whales. Though there is good food supply, these whales cannot feast freely, as they do face numerous threats to their survival.

Since they don't migrate and have a small range, these blue whales are more vulnerable to dangers in their territory, with one of the biggest being large ships. The waters surrounding Sri Lanka are home to one of the busiest shipping lanes in the world. Coming in contact with these vessels can kill blue whales, so Dr. de Vos is on a mission to protect them. How? She uses science to come up with recommendations that have positive benefits for the whale population, the local fishermen, the whale-watching industry, and coastal communities, while not negatively impacting the shipping industry. She believes that solving a conservation problem requires looking at all the pieces of the puzzle.

Ships are not the only threat these whales face. With all the human activity in these waters, blue whales are also at risk of getting entangled in fishing nets, having their lives altered by increasing ocean noises, plastic pollution, oil and gas development, unmanaged whale-watching, and of course, climate change.

THREE DEEP-DIVING MARINE MAMMALS

Many ocean mammals live in the sunlit zone, but dive to significant depths pursuing food or to avoid becoming food themselves.

Sperm whales like those pictured here dive down to hunt big squid species. They can hold their breath for up to an hour and a half and sometimes reach as far as 7,400 feet (2,250 m) below the water's surface. Their heads are also full of a fluid called spermaceti. Researchers think that the fluid hardens into a waxy substance in the cold depths, which may change the whales' buoyancy and help them get back up to the surface.

Elephant seals also hunt in the deep sea. They have a layer of blubber, which keeps them warm in the colder waters, and big eyes so they can see well in the darkness. Southern elephant seals have been tracked swimming as deep as 6,998 feet (2,133 m) and holding their breath underwater for almost two hours. Elephant seals also dive deep to avoid hungry predators such as great white sharks, which hunt seals closer to the surface.

Elephant seals and sperm whales swim far into the ocean depths, but the deep-dive mammal record holder is Cuvier's beaked whale. Scientists tracked one of these whales on a dive that lasted more than two hours on a single breath. The beaked whale made it down to 9,816 feet (2,992 m), which is the length of eight Empire State Buildings stacked one on top of the other!

areas with upwelling (see p. 16). While most dolphin species gather in groups called pods, short-beaked common dolphins gather in pods usually numbering in the hundreds. They have even been observed in what scientists call megapods of at least 10,000 dolphins. Now that's a dolphin party!

POLAR BEAR

This marine mammal is actually one of the biggest predators on land. Measuring up to 8 feet (2.5 m) from nose to tail and weighing up to 1,600 pounds (725 kg), these big bears are apex (or top) predators in the Arctic—that means they have no natural predators in their habitat. They primarily hunt seals. They sniff out seals underneath the ice with their excellent sense of smell, and they're super swimmers, so they can travel from one piece of cracked sea ice to another, looking for seals chilling on ice floes. In fact, in a study of 52 female polar bears, researchers found that 50 of them swam an average long swim of 96 miles (155 km) in a single swimming session. One made it almost 220 miles (354 km) in one long swim.

Even if polar bears are able to cover so much territory, food in the Arctic can be hard to find. To help with the lack of food, a polar bear's metabolism can slow down, meaning the bear can survive longer between meals. But as more Arctic ice melts, some polar bears find it harder to find food.

Other adaptations that help polar bears survive in the harsh conditions of the Arctic are their fur, which even grows on the bottoms of their paws to keep them warm and prevent slipping, and their skin. Underneath all that white fur is black skin to better help soak in the sun's rays to keep the bears warm.

Even polar bear cubs like piggyback rides!

A wandering albatross soars over a bay near South Georgia Island, Antarctica.

A Galápagos penguin perches on a rock.

A BOUNTY OF SEABIRDS

Like marine mammals, seabirds are well adapted to life near, over, and even in the water. With 350 species worldwide, seabirds make up about 3.5 percent of the world's bird species. These birds depend on the ocean for food and spend much of their time flying over or floating or diving in the water, but they rest and nest on land. Seabirds are vulnerable to land and water predators, and like most ocean animals, they're affected by activities such as fishing, but also plastic pollution, habitat destruction, and climate change. In fact, many scientists consider seabirds to be indicator species—animals that, if studied, help us to understand the environmental health of an area, which could mean that a thriving population of seabirds indicates a thriving marine environment. This group of birds includes the amazing wandering albatross and the unique Galápagos penguin.

WANDERING ALBATROSS

My, what a big wingspan you have! The wandering albatross is the biggest of all 22 species of albatrosses, a type of seabird that exists worldwide. Tip to tip, its wingspan can measure up to 11 feet (3.5 m). The birds use their enormous wings to cruise over the ocean for hours at a time. Some large species of albatrosses have been recorded spending five to 10 years traveling at sea.

Wandering albatrosses spend all that time flying over the water looking for food, including fish, squid, and jellyfish. When they spot something that looks good, they dive straight into the water to snatch it up.

When they're not soaring over the ocean in search of food, the wandering albatross is on land, probably nesting. Once these seabirds mate, they stick together for life—which can be up to 50 years.

GALÁPAGOS PENGUIN

Most penguin species live in the southern hemisphere, far south of the Equator, where the weather is cool or very cold. The Galápagos penguin is the only penguin species that lives north of the Equator, in the northern hemisphere. These small penguins are endangered, meaning they are very likely to become extinct. Pollution, climate change, and bycatch in fisheries are three factors that have caused their population to decline.

A female leatherback sea turtle digs a nest on a beach in French Guiana, South America.

To stay cool in their warm island home, they often stand with their flippers outstretched to allow the breeze to move around their bodies. Similar to dogs, these penguins also pant to cool off. Another method they use to beat the heat? Galápagos penguins hunch over in sunlight to shade their feet. These behaviors help them lose heat at a faster rate. And, like people do in hot weather, they will seek out shady spots nearby.

SUPER SEA TURTLES

There are seven species of sea turtles that cruise the waters of the ocean. They are some of the oldest animal species on Earth, having been here for about 110 million years. They once lived alongside dinosaurs! Let's dive into the lives of two super sea turtles.

LEATHERBACK

The largest of all turtles, leatherbacks don't have a hard shell. (Turtle shells are known as a carapace.) They can be found in tropical and temperate waters worldwide, over an area that is greater than where any other species of reptile on Earth roams. Female Western Pacific leatherback sea turtles nest along tropical beaches in places such as Indonesia, Papua New Guinea, and the Solomon Islands. They lay clutches, or groups, of about a hundred eggs on the beaches several times during the nesting season, resting eight to 12 days in between.

After that, some head east to foraging grounds off the western coast of the Americas, particularly the United States.

LEATHERBACK SEA TURTLES ARE THE LARGEST TURTLES IN THE WORLD. THEY REACH LENGTHS OF UP TO SEVEN FEET (2 M) AND WEIGH UP TO 2,000 POUNDS (907 KG).

Their strong flippers help them on one of the longest migrations of any marine animal. This journey of more than 7,000 miles (11,265 km) round-trip takes the turtles 10 months to one year to complete. Along the way, and especially after they arrive, the turtles eat soft-bodied creatures such as jellyfish to give them the energy they'll need to travel back across the ocean to breed and lay eggs again.

A hungry loggerhead crunches on a conch.

LOGGERHEAD

The large, sturdy head of the loggerhead sea turtle holds strong jaw muscles for crunching down on hard-shelled prey. Loggerheads eat horseshoe crabs and other crustaceans, as well as big-shelled conchs. Sometimes they nibble on less crunchy foods like jellyfish and sargassum, a type of brown algae seaweed, that grows at the surface of the water. These turtles range in size from 175 to 400 pounds (79 to 181 kg). They spend nearly all their time in the water, but like all reptiles, they breathe air and need to come to the surface to breathe. Loggerheads live in warm ocean waters worldwide, and they swim long

SEA TURTLES DO NEED TO SURFACE FOR AIR, BUT THEY CAN HOLD THEIR BREATH FOR LONG PERIODS OF TIME UNDERWATER. IN FACT, SOME TURTLES HAVE BEEN TIMED HOLDING THEIR BREATH FOR FOUR TO SEVEN HOURS.

distances. Female loggerheads have been tracked swimming more than 7,500 miles (12,000 km) to lay eggs on the beach where they were hatched.

Females use their back flippers to dig a nest in dry sand where they lay their eggs. A female loggerhead will lay 40 to 190 eggs at a time. The eggs hatch about 60 days later. The hatchlings break out of their shells and dig through the sand, waiting just below the surface until nightfall when they make their way

to the sea. The darkness of night helps the baby turtles avoid dangerous predators such as crabs and seabirds.

Loggerhead turtles are a vulnerable species, meaning they are at risk of becoming endangered. Conservation efforts including the creation of marine protected areas (MPAs), changing fishing techniques, keeping people off of nesting beaches, encouraging locals to eat fewer turtle eggs, and tracking turtles by satellite to help them avoid fisheries are helping to keep loggerheads safe.

FANTASTIC FISH

What lives in the water and has a backbone? That's not the start of a silly joke. Those are the two facts that are true of all fish: They are animals that have a backbone and live in the water. Outside of that, fish species differ widely and wildly. With 32,000 species, there are more species of fish than any other type of vertebrate species on the planet. Here's a peek at just a few fantastic fish.

PARROTFISH

Where there's a coral reef, there's usually a parrotfish. This group of fish live in tropical waters worldwide. Parrotfish get their name from their fused teeth, which form a strong beak that looks like a parrot's. Parrotfish put their beaks to good use. They're coral cleaners. Using their beaks, they scrape algae from coral structures, helping keep the polyps healthy. They also crunch away on dead corals to eat the algae inside, making more room for new polyps to grow. Parrotfish chew up all this hard stuff with strong, molar-like teeth. But these teeth aren't in their mouths—they're plates in their throats that do the grinding.

What happens next may be surprising. Once they're done digesting the algae and corals, parrotfish poop out sand! In fact, one parrotfish can poop out up to 800 pounds

A yellow parrotfish nibbles on coral.

(363 kg) of well-ground white sand in one year. Most of the sand in the areas where parrotfish live is actually from parrotfish releasing the sand as their poop! These fish are seafloor helpers and coral cleaners.

About a hundred species of parrotfish exist worldwide, and they vary in color and size. Even the same type of parrotfish, though, can come in a range of colors and patterns.

AMERICAN EEL

Most marine animals make a seasonal round-trip migration from one area to another, then back again. But the American eel is different. This species of fish migrates only once, as larvae, from salt water to various freshwater sources. Then, as adult eels years later, they head back out to sea to breed, lay eggs, and die. Their migration pattern puts them at risk from pollution, habitat destruction, and climate change, which have had an impact on the eel's population. This fish is now endangered.

American eels lay billions of eggs in the Sargasso Sea. After the eggs hatch, the larvae drift for nine to 12 months in ocean currents, which take them toward freshwater sources along the North American coastline, from Greenland and Iceland south to Venezuela, in South America. The small, see-through larvae—having developed fins and the shape of an adult American eel—then head inland, finding their way to freshwater streams, rivers, and lakes, and to estuaries and lagoons. Because these fish can absorb oxygen through their skin and gills, they are able to travel over land such as wet grass or mud. This helps them cross any barriers between the ocean and inland waters. Their migration can cover more than 3,700 miles (5,955 km), and the journey can take several years.

American eels live in these large freshwater rivers or lakes until they mature, which can take anywhere from 10 to 25 years. Their bodies then slowly undergo several changes before the eels are ready to migrate back to the Sargasso Sea as adults. Since they do not feed while migrating, as they mature, the eel's body fat increases to give them energy for their ocean travels, and their eyes double in size to improve their vision in deep water. Once they return to the Sargasso Sea, the females lay eggs, and then both male and female American eels die. When the new eggs hatch, the cycle begins again.

An adult American eel in Morrison Cave in Florida, U.S.A.

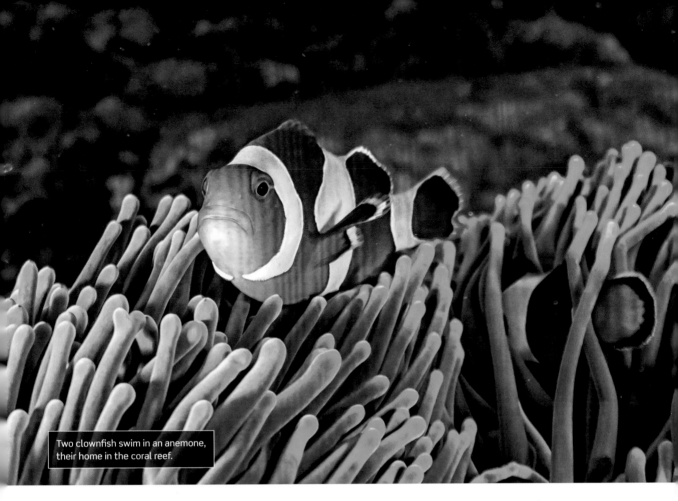

Two clownfish swim in an anemone, their home in the coral reef.

CLOWNFISH

Bright and colorful with stripes of white with black outlines, clownfish might put a smile on your face. These little fish, which grow only about four inches (10 cm) long, are also called anemonefish, because they make their homes in unusual places.

Anemones are invertebrates related to jellyfish, with stinging tentacles and an appetite for fish. But where jellyfish float around the ocean, an anemone attaches itself to rocks or reefs and stays fixed in place. It is in the toxic tentacles of these fish-eaters that clownfish make their homes.

How do clownfish survive the sting? It's thanks to a thick layer of slime that protects the fish from the stinging tentacles of the anemone, and a very important homecoming ritual: When a clownfish checks out a potential anemone home, it very carefully touches the anemone's tentacles with a part of its body. If that feels OK, it touches another part of its body to another tentacle. And it repeats this process a few more times. If everything feels all right, the clownfish has a new home.

NOT ALL CLOWNFISH LOOK LIKE NEMO! AMONG THE 28 SPECIES OF CLOWNFISH, THERE'S A RAINBOW OF COLORS, INCLUDING PINK, RED, YELLOW, AND BROWN.

Often, many clownfish live among one anemone—and the fish and the anemone both get something good from the living arrangement. The fish are protected from other predators that don't want the anemone's painful—sometimes deadly—sting. And the clownfish eats parasites off of the anemone. It's an awesome setup.

THE SUPER SARGASSO

The Sargasso Sea is a two-million-square-mile (5.2 million-sq-km) expanse of open ocean in the Atlantic. It is the only sea in the world that doesn't have a land boundary. Instead, it's bordered by ocean currents. How can you recognize this large stretch of sea? Sargassum, a species of free-floating brown algae seaweed, grows and floats atop the warm waters. These carpets of vegetation house an abundance of wildlife, many of which have adapted to the seaweed. They act as nurseries for turtle hatchlings, which use the seaweed as both shelter and a source of food. The sargassum fish, pictured here and named for the algae that it lives in and resembles, swims through the seaweed stalks. It can even survive out of water for short periods of time, lying on the brown mats of algae to escape predators. Humpback whales swim though this area on their migrations, and even migrating seabirds depend on the Sargasso Sea for food.

INCREDIBLE INVERTEBRATES

Invertebrates are animals without a backbone. Invertebrates make up about 97 percent of all animals on Earth. They live in all types of habitats worldwide, and the ocean is full of them too. Marine invertebrates include everything from marine worms to mollusks, a group that encompasses octopuses as well as mussels and clams. Crabs, sponges, echinoderms like starfish and urchins, jellyfish, anemones, corals, and more are also in this group. Let's take a look at some of these incredible invertebrates.

NUDIBRANCH

With as many hues as a jumbo box of markers, the colorful nudibranch is a spectacular undersea sight. There are some 3,000 species of these sea slug relatives, and they can be as small as the tip of your thumb or up to a foot (30 cm) long. Nudibranchs get their wild colors from what they eat: anemones, corals, sponges, barnacles—and even each other. As they digest a colorful food source, their food's

You are what you eat! A nudibranch's colors can change depending on what it eats.

color shows up in the nudibranch itself.

Nudibranchs breathe through body parts on their backs, either through organs called cerata or gills that stick out like feathers. Nudibranchs feel around for prey using the antennae-like tentacles on their heads. As gastropods, these squishy-bodied sea slugs are related to snails. But how do they protect themselves without a shell? Some types of nudibranchs absorb venom from the stinging prey they eat, such as anemones, and let it ooze from their skin. If a fish takes a bite of a nudibranch, they'll regret it.

MIMIC OCTOPUS
First observed in 1998 off the coast of Sulawesi, Indonesia, in the Pacific Ocean, the mimic octopus is a newly discovered cephalopod (a group of invertebrates that includes octopuses, nautiluses, squid, and cuttlefish). So we don't yet know much about this creature. Especially because it likes to disguise itself as other animals. So far, scientists have counted up to 10 disguises mimic octopuses have perfected. Every one of these acts help the octopuses hide in plain sight or deter potential predators.

For example, mimic octopuses can flatten themselves into a leaf shape to mimic the banded sole, a type of venomous flatfish. But the mimic octopus doesn't just *look* like a banded sole. It *moves* like one too, acting out the fish's rippling swimming motion.

One of the most venomous animals in the world is the banded sea krait, a type of undersea snake that can burrow into the sandy seafloor. The mimic octopus has the snake's act down too: The octopus will slide six of its arms and its body into a hole and wave the

THERE ARE ABOUT 300 DIFFERENT KNOWN SPECIES OF OCTOPUS. THE LARGEST IS THE GIANT PACIFIC OCTOPUS, WHICH CAN WEIGH UP TO 600 POUNDS (272 KG).

other two arms outside of the hole around like a slithery snake. The octopus's banding looks just like the dangerous sea krait's. Other disguises include a venomous lionfish and also crabs, shrimp, and even anemones.

LINED CHITON
There's a lot of algae in the ocean. Luckily, there are a lot of algae eaters. Here's one that looks like a patch of pink armor stuck to a rock. Underneath that pink armor is a soft-bodied mollusk called the lined chiton.

A mimic octopus blends into the sand on the seafloor.

Lined chitons attach to rocks covered in algae.

Lined chitons feed on coralline algae, which forms thick, crusty pink patches on the tops of rocks. Lined chitons slowly slide over the crusty algae using a foot, much like a snail's, while munching on the top of the algae along with much smaller organisms that are also feeding on the algae.

ALGAE CAN BE USED TO MAKE FUEL. IN 2011 CONTINENTAL AIRLINES FLIGHT 1403 WAS THE FIRST PASSENGER FLIGHT IN THE U.S. TO BE POWERED BY BIOFUEL MADE FROM ALGAE.

Their pink armor, etched with diagonal lines, camouflages them so they're hard to see against the pink coralline algae they eat so much of. Blending in helps keep them safe from their top predators: sea stars and otters. Lined chitons are found in cool waters off the Pacific Northwest of the United States and southern Alaska in intertidal zones and waters up to 300 feet (90 m) deep.

HELMET JELLYFISH

Floating in the depths of the midnight zone is the red-colored helmet jellyfish. Like many deep-sea creatures, they are bioluminescent—they're able to light up, perhaps to communicate with each other or to either attract or avoid becoming prey. But they definitely don't like sunlight: they've been observed swimming away from it.

The bell or cone of these jellies can grow to about a foot (30 cm) in diameter, with nearly eight-inch (20-cm) orange tentacles trailing behind.

Though helmet jellies like the deep, dark sea, they have been seen swimming to shallower depths at night, perhaps to feed. These invertebrates can also swarm in large numbers—so large, in fact, that in areas of Norway, they're threatening local fishing operations by eating young fish and the food those young fish need to survive, including krill and small crustaceans known as copepods.

The helmet jelly's red bell stands out in dark waters.

KRILL

Krill are very small crustaceans that look like shrimp. They are a bit bigger than plankton, measuring about two inches (5 cm) long. These little critters feed on phytoplankton and need sunshine to survive, and like plankton, they're a huge link in the food chain. Krill, like many types of zooplankton, stay in the deeper waters of the twilight zone during the day and migrate upward at night. This may help them avoid being eaten by large predators.

There are about 85 species of krill. One kind, Antarctic krill, forms groups so dense that they can be seen from space! They alone may amount to six billion tons of food for baleen whales, including humpbacks, blue whales, and minke whales, and for penguins, crabeater seals, squid, and other animals in the waters around Antarctica.

Of the many animals that feed on krill,

Antarctic krill are tiny but they are a food source for some of the largest marine animals in the world.

baleen whales—a group of whale species with filtering plates, rather than teeth, in their mouths—especially like them. Blue whales, for example, can consume more than two tons (1.8 t) of krill in a single day. Baleen whales will scoop up whole patches of krill with their mouths, then use their tongues to press the water through the baleen plates. The plates filter the water back out but trap the krill inside, which the whales then swallow.

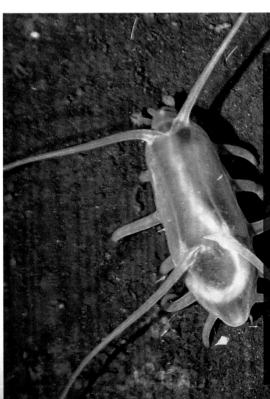

SEA PIGS

Sea pigs are actually a type of sea cucumber—and not related to pigs or cucumbers at all. These see-through pink walking blobs are close cousins of sea stars and urchins, and like their cousins, they live deep in the ocean, on the seafloor. Sea pigs trudge along the seafloor on tube-like feet. Even the body parts that look like antennae function as feet, to help them balance and move around.

About four to six inches (10 to 15 cm) long, these animals pick through the deep-sea mud for decayed bits of plants and animals, which they suck up with their tentacled mouth. If sea pigs find a particularly yummy spot of mud or a decaying animal to nibble on, they can gather in groups to eat it up.

Squishy and blob-like though they may be, sea pigs can protect themselves: They have toxins in their skin that keep predators from taking more than one bite.

SURPRISING SHARKS

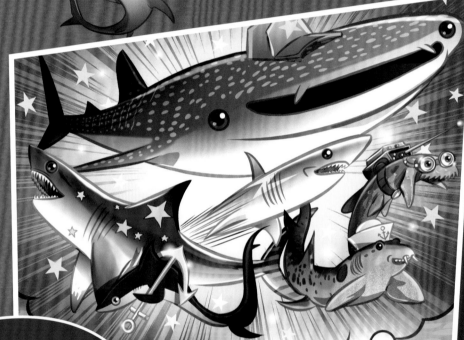

SURPRISING SHARKS

Sharks have existed on Earth for a long time: about one hundred times longer than hominids, or humans and our closest relatives—and two hundred million years longer than the dinosaurs. Dinosaurs first showed up about 240 million years ago. And the first sharks, such as *Leonodus*, appeared in the oceans nearly 200 million years *before* that; the first fossils date back to at least 425 million years ago.

Sharks have survived so long because they have been able to adapt to changing conditions on Earth and to many different habitats. For example, about 250 million years ago, nine out of ten marine species went extinct. Scientists don't know what caused this event, called the Great Dying—they think it was likely due to climate change or volcanic activity—but they do know that sharks remained on the planet. How do they know this? By studying the fossilized teeth of a shark relative, scientists determined that these sharks swam to deeper ocean waters, ably adjusting both their environment and their diet in order to survive.

Today's sharks are just as unique and impressive as their early relatives. Let's take a look at a few exceptional species of sharks.

A fossilized tooth of *Carcharopsis wortheni*. The blue lines represent where blood would have flowed through the tooth.

SCIENTIST PROFILE

Allison Bronson

Dr. Allison Bronson uses x-rays to study the anatomy of fossilized sharks. Some of Dr. Bronson's research focuses on *Carcharopsis wortheni*, a 320-million-year-old shark that lived after the End-Devonian Hangenberg mass extinction event. This event took place about 360 million years ago when about 80 percent of the animals that lived during the Devonian period died out.

Dr. Bronson studied the first ever cranium of this shark. It was a rare find because sharks are made of cartilage, which doesn't fossilize easily. Before this finding, all the evidence we had of *Carcharopsis wortheni* were parts of its jaws and teeth.

The fossils of some early shark relatives are truly bizarre. The jaws of *Helicoprion*, a shark-like sea creature, was spiral-shaped.

Fossilized teeth, which are sometimes the only fossils found of a former shark, can be helpful clues to how the animal once lived. These preserved remains of what used to catch and kill prey can help scientists answer where sharks lived and what they ate, and how big they grew. *Carcharopsis wortheni* had serrated teeth—like the edge of a saw blade—a feature rarely found in early shark specimens but common in modern sharks. Using high-resolution computed tomography (CT) imaging, the scientists discovered that the internal canals and arrangement of blood vessels in this shark's teeth suggest that it was probably related to a group of ancient fish that included crown elasmobranchs and an extinct group of sharks called hybodonts, from which today's sharks evolved. The teeth are about an inch and a half (4 cm) long—but they revealed a huge discovery!

A shark can lose thousands of teeth in its lifetime, providing scientists with plenty of fossils that help identify ancient sharks. Some prehistoric sharks are known only by the size and shape of their teeth.

Great white sharks are ambush predators. They often surprise sea lions by attacking from below.

THE GREAT WHITE

Perhaps the best known shark in the world is the great white. Adult great whites average about 15 feet (4.6 m) in length and can weigh up to 5,000 pounds (2,270 kg). These torpedo-shaped ambush predators use their powerful tail, or caudal, fins to reach short-burst speeds of 30 miles an hour (48 km/h). Great whites are partially warm-blooded, which means they can raise their body temperature to that of the water in different climates, allowing them bursts of speed to hunt in both cooler and warmer waters. They generally attack prey from below. When they rush up under an unsuspecting seal or sea lion, they can strike so hard that both prey and predator launch out of the water as the shark attempts to grab its meal. At two inches (5 cm) long, great white sharks have the largest teeth of any living shark species, and one of the most powerful bites in the animal kingdom. Their amazing sense of smell can sniff out one drop of blood in 10 billion drops of water (that's about one drop of blood in a body of water that is roughly the size of an Olympic swimming pool), and with their small but sensitive ears, they can pick up even the tiniest vibration in the water.

These apex, or top, predators are named for their white underbellies, but they have also been called white death or maneater, nicknames that don't help dispel the image of the bloodthirsty and flesh-eating creature featured in the 1975 film *Jaws*. In reality, great whites are very intelligent and actually rather picky about what they eat. Careful and cautious hunters, they often take an exploratory bite of an object to determine its tastiness before launching a full attack.

People actually pose more of a threat to great whites than they do to us. The International Union for Conservation of

Great whites, like all sharks, have rows of replacement teeth that shift into an empty space whenever a tooth falls out.

Nature categorizes them as a vulnerable species, which means they are likely to become endangered with possible extinction if the circumstances threatening their survival do not

BABY GREAT WHITE SHARKS ARE CALLED PUPS, AND THEY CAN BE BORN IN GROUPS OF AS MANY AS 10 PUPS AT A TIME. GREAT WHITE PUPS SWIM AWAY FROM THEIR MOTHERS AT BIRTH AND TAKE CARE OF THEMSELVES.

improve. Great whites are caught both by fishing vessels and in nets that are placed along coastlines to keep them away from shallow waters and beaches. They (and many other sharks) are also caught for their meat, liver oil, and fins, which are used for shark-fin soup, considered a delicacy in some countries.

Great whites' only known ocean predator is the orca, or killer whale. How do orcas attack and kill such a fierce predator? One way is to ram into the side of a great white,

Orcas are excellent hunters and the only known predator of great white sharks. Here, an orca attacks a porpoise.

briefly stunning it. The orca then flips it over on its back, a position that makes the shark unable to move. Once the shark is essentially helpless, the orcas can consume what they want. But even after all that work, orcas have been observed to eat just the great white's liver, which is filled with oil that sharks use to regulate their buoyancy in the ocean. Researchers think this is because shark livers are large—typically accounting for between 8 and 16 percent of a shark's total body weight—and are a good energy source for the orcas.

Though great whites are a well-known species in popular culture, there is still much to discover about them. The best way to do that is observing how great whites live in their natural habitat. Using tags that can communicate via satellite, researchers have begun to estimate the number of the great whites worldwide. They are also getting a better idea of where the great whites swim and why they go to certain areas at different times of the year.

Once a year, groups of great whites head to the middle of the Pacific Ocean to a location that scientists call the White Shark Café, about halfway between California and Hawaii. Scientists aren't entirely sure what the sharks do there. The area—which is about the same size as Colorado, U.S.A.—is very isolated; it is roughly 1,200 miles (1,930 km) from the coastline, where white sharks normally hang out. What researchers do know is that, while there, the great whites regularly dive thousands of feet deep, with males diving and rising quickly up to 120 times each day and females diving deep during the day and rising at night. Researchers suppose that the sharks may go to this spot to engage in complex courtship and mating behaviors, and possibly to feed.

CAUGHT ON CAMERA

Imagine you're in an underwater diving cage, and a great white shark, 20 feet (6 m) long and as wide as a small elephant, swims by, close enough to touch. That's just what happened to a group of scientists off the coast of Guadalupe Island, near Mexico. As a female shark circled their enclosure, their video cameras caught her in action. Nicknamed Deep Blue, she was believed to be the biggest great white shark ever filmed. The photo here is a still from those video cameras.

Deep Blue was more than just an internet sensation and a camera-catching record holder, however; for the scientists, she was a hopeful indication of the effectiveness of protection and conservation efforts. It takes decades for great whites to reach adult size, so a behemoth like Deep Blue is likely an older shark—scientists estimated that she is about 50 years old. Also, she wasn't just longer than the average great white; her wide girth indicated pregnancy. Scientists think great whites can live to about 60 years of age, and once females reach maturity at about age 17, they can reproduce for the rest of their lives. Bigger sharks are more likely to produce bigger litters too, so larger females like Deep Blue are critical in helping the great white shark population thrive. One scientist estimated that Deep Blue could have given birth to almost 200 pups over her lifetime.

THE MIGHTY MEGALODON

About 16 million years ago, a monster shark species roamed the seas. Megalodon may have looked and acted very much like the great white of today, but this ancient shark was much bigger and was not a close relative of the great white shark. The megalodon grew to 50 feet (16 m) or more in length—that's more than double the length of the largest great white. It also had teeth like the one pictured here, which could grow up to seven inches (18 cm) long! Its bite force is estimated to have been 24,000 to 40,000 pounds (10,900 to 18,145 kg), much stronger than any other creature that ever lived, including *Tyrannosaurus rex*, which had a bite force of about 6,834 pounds (3,100 kg). Megalodon's bite was strong enough to crush something the size of a small car!

A HAMMER FOR A HEAD

A hammerhead shark's flattened, elongated head is a specialized meal detector. Its eyes sit at either end of its uniquely shaped head, giving a hammerhead excellent vision to scan the ocean waters for fish, squid, and other prey. Living creatures give off tiny electrical pulses, and all sharks have specialized jelly-filled pores called ampullae of Lorenzini that pick up these pulses. Hammerheads take this sense to the next level. Their ampullae of Lorenzini run along the length of their heads, and this greater surface area means they have more of these electroreceptors than other types of sharks. These sensors also come in handy in dark, deep water, where the prowling hammerhead's wide-set eyes wouldn't be helpful in spotting prey. This sixth sense, as scientists sometimes call it, is why a hammerhead's favorite meal, a stingray, can't stay hidden under the sand for long! The shark locates it, then uses its head to pin the stingray to the seafloor and immobilizes it with a bite to the pectoral fin. The shark also uses its head for steering, like a rudder.

The 10 species in the hammerhead family vary in size. The smaller ones range from three to five feet (0.9 to 1.5 m) in length, while the largest, the great hammerhead, can be up to 20 feet (6 m) long and weigh more than a thousand pounds (450 kg).

One of the most unique species of hammerhead sharks is the winghead. Relative to its body size, the winghead shark has the widest head of any hammerhead—almost half as wide as its body is long.

Winghead sharks are endangered, facing multiple threats to their survival. Their distinctive head shape lends itself to entanglement in fishing nets near shorelines. People also target them both for food and for their livers, which are used to make oil and vitamins.

Another type of hammerhead, the scalloped hammerhead, can travel great distances in large schools, which make them an easy target for large fishing nets. The great hammerhead often swims alone and can be caught on a variety of fishing gear near shorelines.

Hammerheads, like other sharks, are not only targeted for their fins. They're often targeted for their meat, which is an important source of protein in some countries. Unfortunately, like all shark species, hammerheads reproduce slowly. This means that human activity is reducing their populations faster than the sharks can produce offspring.

A scalloped hammerhead swims in the Red Sea near Egypt.

This makes their populations go down, which makes them vulnerable to extinction. But scientists have learned which species of sharks are being fished too quickly, and they're working hard to help protect hammerheads and others that need it.

SPEEDY SWIMMER

Shortfin mako sharks are the cheetahs of the sea. These sharks, sometimes called torpedoes with teeth, are built for extreme speed. They can swim as fast as burst speeds of 35 miles an hour (56 km/h). Shortfin makos feed mainly on bluefish, but they sometimes target tuna, which can travel almost as fast as

their predators, at 25 miles an hour (40 km/h). Like great whites, makos are so fast that they sometimes burst out of the water when attacking prey, leaping up to 40 feet (12 m) in the air.

SCALLOPED HAMMERHEADS SWIM IN HUGE SCHOOLS OF A HUNDRED OR MORE SHARKS.

Makos' streamlined bodies have dense muscles, which keep these sharks from tiring out during a long chase. Unlike most sharks, whose tails are powered by red muscles running along their body, a mako's red muscles are located closer to the backbone. This design, combined with short pectoral fins and a pointed nose that reduces drag in the water, improves their ability to move with speed and force.

SUPER SURVIVOR

Known as an aggressive species, bull sharks, pound for pound, have the strongest bite of any living shark, out-chomping even great whites and tiger sharks. They can easily crush

A mako shark speeds through the open ocean.

A close-up view of a bull shark shows the small dots along its snout. These are its ampullae of Lorenzini, organs that all sharks have. The organs help sharks sense prey.

materials such as bones and turtle shells. Like the land mammal they were named after, bull sharks sometimes use their short, blunt snout to head-butt their prey in an effort to stun their victims. These sharks have very small eyes, but because they spend a lot of time in murky waters, sight isn't a sense they need to rely on.

Unlike most shark species, which are adapted to salt water, bull sharks can survive and even thrive in both saltwater and freshwater environments. How do they do it? Their kidneys can adjust to the amount of salt in the water by removing more salt in salt water and less salt in freshwater to maintain a healthy balance. Bull sharks hunt mainly fish in freshwater, but they're not picky eaters.

THE TAIL'S IN CHARGE

Thresher sharks are sleek swimmers found in temperate and tropical ocean waters. The bottom lobe of their caudal fin, or tail fin, is about the same length as any similarly sized shark's. But the top lobe trails behind the shark up to more than half its body length. Some of the longest thresher tails measure about 20 feet (6 m).

Thresher sharks have weak jaws and relatively small teeth, so instead of using their mouth to catch fish, their primary food source, they use their extralong tail to corral them into a tight bunch. Then the threshers dash through the fish and flick their caudal fin, the tip of which strikes prey at incredible speeds—just like the tip of a whip—stunning

A common thresher shark patrols the waters near the Philippines.

or even killing the prey. Then threshers circle back to swallow their meal.

There is so much more to learn about these incredible sharks. Scientists, including those who are part of the Thresher Shark Project, are trying to study and understand more about them.

GENTLE GIANTS

The largest shark in the world eats the smallest organisms. Swimming close to the ocean's surface with its five-foot (1.5-m)-wide mouth gaping open, the whale shark looks like it is on the hunt for a bicycle-size fish. Though it could fit one in its jaws, these slow movers

The whale shark is the largest fish in the sea.

are instead looking for plankton, or even some small fish that happen to be in their path. Whale sharks, like basking sharks and megamouth sharks, are filter feeders, filtering their meals out of enormous amounts of water. Whale and megamouth sharks use muscles in their head to actively suck in water, while basking sharks passively swim around, mouths wide open. Either way, the water passes through their gills, where net-

> EVEN THOUGH THEY'RE FILTER FEEDERS, WHALE SHARKS HAVE 300 TO 350 ROWS OF TINY TEETH IN THEIR HUGE MOUTHS.

like pads called gill rakers catch their food. The shark then shuts its mouth and swallows its teeny-tiny prey. Young whale sharks can eat about 46 pounds (21 kg) of food each day.

Whale sharks can grow to be as long as 40 feet (12 m), but they are gentle giants.

COOL CAMOUFLAGE

Wobbegongs are a family of sharks with a pattern on their skin that resembles a rug, which is why they are often called carpet sharks. This pattern and thin whisker-like lobes around their mouths allow them to blend in with the ocean floor, protecting them from predators. Their camouflage also helps hide wobbegongs from unsuspecting prey. These ambush predators lie still on the ocean floor, waiting until a hungry fish swims by and mistakes the shark's "mustache" for strands of algae. That's when the wobbegong strikes, quickly clamping down on prey with wide, powerful jaws. Sometimes, the shark sucks in almost the entire prey by quickly expanding its throat as it opens its mouth.

Like nurse sharks and angel sharks, wobbegongs are able to pump water through their mouths and over their gills using strong cheek muscles. Unlike most other sharks, which have to swim to breathe through their

A wobbegong shark blends into its surroundings.

gills, wobbegongs (and nurse sharks) can breathe while remaining motionless. These sharks sometimes use their pectoral fins to "climb" over rocks between tide pools in search of food. As long as their gills remain wet, they can survive for the short time it takes to get to the next pool.

JUST A BITE?

Cookiecutter sharks get their name from the cookie-size holes they bite out of prey much larger than themselves. Though they are less than two feet (0.6 m) long, these sharks have the largest teeth relative to body size of any shark species. During the day, these small sharks stay very deep underwater, sometimes as far down as 3,281 feet (1,000 m). At night, they swim closer to the surface, up to about 300 feet (90 m) deep. There, these bioluminescent animals create their own light, giving off a greenish glow. The shark's light attracts predators like tuna, bigger sharks, seals, and dolphins. But just when

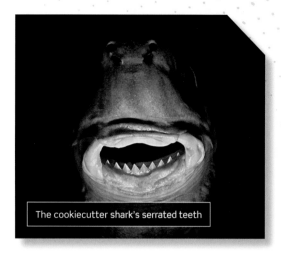

The cookiecutter shark's serrated teeth

those larger predators think they have a meal, the cookiecutter shark swerves sideways and attaches itself to its prey with suction-cup lips. Like a can opener, it spins around to slice out a circular chunk of meat, then swims away. These bites are not fatal for the larger animals, but it's just enough for the cookiecutter shark to fill its belly and escape the predator.

TRY THIS
Unsinkable Sharks

1 Use a permanent marker to draw a shark or shark face on each bottle.

2 Fill one water bottle with oil and the other water bottle with water and replace the caps.

3 Fill the bowl with water.

4 Set both bottles into the bowl of water.

5 Watch what happens. The shark bottle with oil should float and the shark bottle with water should sink.

Materials:
- Permanent marker
- Two 8-ounce (237 mL) water bottles
- Cooking oil
- Water
- 12-inch (30-cm) bowl (or container large enough to hold the two water bottles with room to spare)

What You Learned
Oil is less dense than water, so it is able to float. When you pour both oil and water into a container, the oil rises to the top and creates a thin layer. Oil is what allows sharks to float rather than sink in water. Sharks have high oil content in their livers, which means their livers are light and buoyant. Sharks' livers serve as a kind of floating device, keeping them from sinking as they swim from place to place. Most other fish have gas-filled swim bladders that keep them afloat.

chapter 8

UNDERWATER TECHNOLOGY

UNDERWATER TECHNOLOGY

In 1872 a ship named the H.M.S. *Challenger* set out on what is now considered the first oceanographic expedition to collect scientific data on the world's oceans and its marine life. Over the course of the three-and-a-half-

> THE *CHALLENGER* WAS A 200-FOOT (61-M) BRITISH NAVY SHIP. MOST OF ITS GUN BAYS WERE CONVERTED TO LABS AND STOREROOMS FOR THE SCIENTISTS' EQUIPMENT.

year voyage, scientists aboard the ship learned how currents move water through the oceans, and discovered the Mariana Trench

and more than 4,700 species of marine plants and animals. It took another 19 years to compile a 50-volume report on their findings—data that is still referenced today.

The scientists aboard used trawls and nets to capture animals and samples from the seafloor, and a hundred-pound (45-kg) weight attached to a rope to measure the ocean's depths. Since the *Challenger*'s historic voyage, underwater technology has come a long way. From super sonar to scuba gear and submersibles, let's take a look at how scientists today are exploring Earth's vast oceans.

A photo of the crew of the H.M.S. *Challenger*, taken during their 1872 expedition

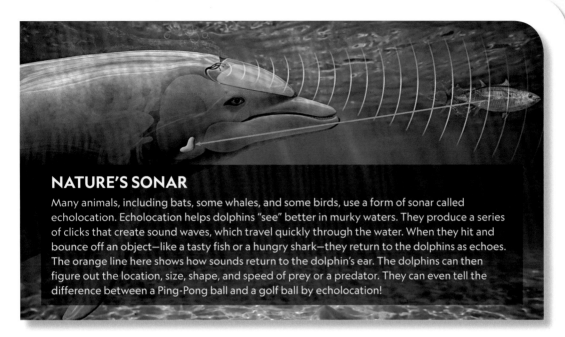

NATURE'S SONAR

Many animals, including bats, some whales, and some birds, use a form of sonar called echolocation. Echolocation helps dolphins "see" better in murky waters. They produce a series of clicks that create sound waves, which travel quickly through the water. When they hit and bounce off an object—like a tasty fish or a hungry shark—they return to the dolphins as echoes. The orange line here shows how sounds return to the dolphin's ear. The dolphins can then figure out the location, size, shape, and speed of prey or a predator. They can even tell the difference between a Ping-Pong ball and a golf ball by echolocation!

SUPER SONAR

In the early 1900s, a technology called sonar was invented. Sonar, short for sound navigation and ranging, uses the movement of sound to measure distance and to find objects underwater. Ocean scientists primarily use two types of sonar to study the seafloor or other underwater environments: multibeam echo sounders and side-scan sonar. Multibeam sonar measures the depth of the seafloor and helps scientists map it. The sonar device is mounted to the bottom of a boat, and it sends out a series of ping-like sound waves into the depths. The device tracks the amount of time it takes for the sound waves to travel from the ship to the seafloor, then echo back up to the boat. The longer the waves take to go down and come back, the deeper that part of the ocean. Using this data, researchers can create maps of the ocean floor. The maps often use colors to show different depths and seafloor features, such as trenches, ridges, and submerged islands.

Side-scan sonar is generally used to find objects. It measures the strength of the returning echoes, rather than the time it takes for the echoes to return. This device is usually towed behind a research ship and creates black-and-white photo-like images of the seafloor. Hard areas like rock return stronger echoes that appear as darker spots on the image, and soft areas like sand produce

A marine biologist studies a map of the seafloor created using sonar.

Jess Cramp checks out the rocky bottom of a lagoon.

weaker echoes that show up as lighter spots. Researchers use side-scan sonar to search for ship and plane wrecks, and fishers use it to locate schools of fish.

DIVING IN!

Scuba gear ("scuba" is short for self-contained underwater breathing apparatus) allows researchers to stay underwater and study

TO BE ABLE TO SCUBA DIVE, YOU NEED TO COMPLETE A SERIES OF CLASSES AND BECOME CERTIFIED. KIDS AS YOUNG AS 10 CAN GET THEIR SCUBA CERTIFICATION!

marine creatures without needing to surface to breathe. Divers wear a wetsuit, a mask, and fins, and carry a tank of compressed air on their back that weighs about 30 pounds (13 kg). Underwater, these heavy tanks feel almost weightless. Divers take breaths using a regulator, which connects to the tank by a hose. The regulator reduces the pressure from the tank to a level safe for the diver to inhale, and it supplies air whenever the diver takes a breath. The air in the tank is about 75 percent nitrogen and 25 percent oxygen, much like the atmospheric air we breathe on land. Depending on the size and experience of the diver, a person can stay underwater for over an hour on a single tank of air!

UNDERWATER VIDEO

Another tool that researchers use to learn about life beneath the waves is a baited remote underwater video station, or BRUV. One or more cameras are attached to these stations, with a bag of bait in view of the camera. The stations themselves either float or are anchored to the seafloor. They are used to survey the size, abundance, and diversity of fish species in a given location. They are particularly helpful in determining the presence of marine species that are normally shy around divers.

Jess Cramp employs BRUV stations to identify shark density and diversity in specific locations. Using these in the South Pacific, Cramp

A diver swims to the seafloor to place a BRUV.

discovered one of the highest densities of gray reef sharks in the world. The sharks swim around Beveridge Reef, an uninhabited atoll, or ring-shaped coral reef, that is part of a small Pacific Island country called Niue. Cramp's findings will help create a large marine protected area (MPA) around parts of Niue and Beveridge Reef, so it will become a refuge for these sharks and all other marine life in the area.

LISTENING TO THE OCEAN

The ocean isn't a quiet place. Many marine animals use sound to communicate, reproduce, and find prey. Undersea earthquakes and volcanoes rumble on the ocean floor. To hear what's going on beneath the water's surface, scientists use a hydrophone, or underwater microphone. Just as microphones collect sound waves in air, hydrophones pick up sound waves in the ocean. They can be used individually to amplify sounds, or multiple devices can be positioned—even thousands of miles apart—to provide even greater sound sensitivity and to determine the direction from which sound is coming.

While scientists use hydrophones to eavesdrop on baleen whales singing and dolphins whistling, they also hope to use these devices to learn where marine animals need protection in their underwater homes. For example, an array of hydrophones anchored to the

The ship the *Trieste*, which was designed by Auguste Piccard

seafloor along high-traffic shipping lanes in the Atlantic Ocean alert ship captains when an endangered right whale is nearby. The captain can then steer clear of the whale's swimming space, making it less likely that the ship will injure or kill the whale in a collision.

Jess Cramp is part of a team of National Geographic Explorers, including Shah Selbe and Topher White, who are developing a solar-powered hydrophone buoy that could be dropped off in MPAs. The hydrophone aims to tell the difference between the sounds of various boats and fishing gear in order to identify illegal fishing activities. This technology could help communities police their MPAs and save vulnerable species.

DEEPWATER TRANSPORTATION

In 1930 two Americans, undersea explorer Charles William Beebe and engineer Otis Barton, made history, descending 1,426 feet (435 m) beneath the ocean's surface near Bermuda in a submersible, an underwater vehicle. Called the bathysphere, this 4,500-pound (2,041-kg) cast-iron sphere of Barton's design was a cozy ride at less than five feet (1.5 m) wide. It had a large hatch on one side and three small portholes, or windows, on the opposite side. Beebe's and Barton's descent was the deepest ever; until then, no one had descended deeper than 350 feet (107 m) and survived. Their underwater trip was broadcast live on the radio as listeners heard Beebe describe the "brilliant light" of a school of jellyfish just three feet (0.9 m) from his window. Two years later, Beebe and Barton squeezed into the bathysphere and set a record again, sinking 3,028 feet (923 m)—twice as deep as their first dive—and documenting deep-sea creatures no human had ever seen.

More than two decades later, explorers surpassed Beebe's and Barton's records. For years, Swiss balloon pilot and builder Auguste Piccard had been designing underwater vessels that he called bathyscaphes, which means "deep ships." In 1958 the United

The *Alvin*, on an expedition in 1978

Explorer-at-Large James Cameron continued the work that Walsh and Piccard had begun 50 years earlier. The first person to make the trip solo, Cameron guided the *DEEPSEA CHALLENGER*, a single-seat submersible, to Challenger Deep. From inside his sphere-shaped pilot's chamber—a space so small that he was unable to extend his arms—Cameron spent almost three hours filming footage and collecting rocks and creatures from the ocean floor with the vessel's mechanical arm.

The cameras caught large numbers of a previously unknown species of sea cucumber camouflaged against the sandy seafloor. Like sea stars, sea cucumbers use tube feet that look like tentacles to catch food as it drifts by. The ones that appeared on Cameron's footage looked frozen in place and faced the same direction, presumably to help catch as much as possible from the few food-bearing currents that reach their waving tube feet in the trench. Microbial mats—dark brown, carpet-like clumps of microorganisms—sprouted from rocks on the seafloor, and amphipods, which are shrimplike crustaceans, looked like snow-flakes. Cameron's expedition revealed exciting discoveries about the deepest spot on Earth.

States Navy purchased one of these submersibles. The *Trieste* was meant to go deeper than any other underwater vehicle available at the time. In 1960 American oceanographer Don Walsh and Swiss oceanographer Jacques Piccard eventually landed the vessel 36,000 feet (10,980 m) down in Challenger Deep—the deepest part of the Mariana Trench, a canyon in the western Pacific seafloor, and the deepest point on Earth's surface. It is so deep that Mount Everest, at 29,035 feet (8,850 m), would disappear under the water—with more than 6,000 feet (1,830 m) to spare—if you dropped it into Challenger Deep!

The *Trieste* was the first vessel to make it to the bottom of the Mariana Trench, but it was not equipped to take photographs or collect samples, and it rested in the trench for only 20 minutes before ascending to the ocean's surface. In 2012 National Geographic

MORE PEOPLE HAVE BEEN TO THE MOON THAN HAVE BEEN TO THE DEEPEST PARTS OF THE SEA.

Another deep-sea research submersible, *Alvin*, wins the record for the most dives: more than 4,800. First tested in 1964, *Alvin* can carry two scientists and one pilot 14,760 feet (4,500 m) into the ocean's depths and stay submerged for up to nine hours. It can maneuver around rugged seascapes and hover in place like a helicopter so that researchers can perform experiments or take photographs or video.

In 1974 researchers aboard *Alvin* confirmed the theory of seafloor spreading along the Mid-Atlantic Ridge. Three years later, *Alvin* carried oceanographer and National Geographic Explorer-at-Large Robert Ballard to the Galápagos Rift in the Pacific Ocean to search for hydrothermal vents, deep-sea hot springs that form when cracks in the ocean floor allow cold ocean water to seep down into the Earth. Earth's hot magma core heats up the water, which reaches temperatures of up to 700°F (370°C). The water, now mixed with chemicals from Earth's core, spurts back up into the ocean. Ballard and his team expected to find a lifeless desert, but they were shocked to discover that these seemingly uninhabitable vents were teeming with never before seen creatures: giant clams, blind crabs, tiny eyeless shrimp, and colorful tube worms. They also discovered these animals' food source: bacteria. The water from the vents contains chemicals that feed the bacteria, which then support this unique oasis of life in Earth's darkest depths.

A photo of a hydrothermal vent, taken from the *Alvin*

ROVING INTO IMPORTANT DISCOVERIES

Some places in the ocean, such as shipwreck sites, underwater caves, and deep-sea habitats, are difficult and dangerous for a human to explore. Time to bring in the robots! Remotely operated vehicles (ROVs) are underwater robots that can tell researchers a lot about the ocean. Scientists operate them from the surface, usually aboard a ship. Cables carry signals from the ship down to the ROV and from the ROV back up to the ship.

Diana Garcia-Benito

Growing up in Venezuela, South America, on a farm in the jungle far from the ocean, Spanish scientist Diana Garcia-Benito always dreamed of becoming a submarine pilot. She had read and loved Jules Verne's book *20,000 Leagues Under the Sea*, in which the main character captains the *Nautilus* through many underwater adventures. Years later, after working hard to earn opportunities in a male-dominated field, she achieved her childhood goal, becoming the first commercial female submarine pilot. Her submarine dives take her past deep-sea jellyfish, sharks, and bioluminescent plankton. Garcia-Benito is also a free diver, which means she explores deep underwater without a snorkel or scuba gear and simply holds her breath. She's an instructor, and also holds a Spanish national free-diving record. She is also the founder of the DeepChange Project, an organization that helps educate and raise awareness about the fundamental role Earth's oceans play on our planet.

An image of the *Titanic*, captured during the 1985 expedition

Ocean explorer Robert Ballard used an unmanned machine similar to an ROV but that is towed behind another vessel to locate shipwrecks, including the *Titanic*. In 1985 Ballard was working with teams of French scientists and researchers for Woods Hole Oceanographic Institution, searching for sunken military submarines from aboard a ship, which towed a sled that carried a system of television cameras and sonars. The sled system, called *Argo*, helped Ballard locate two subs. Thanks to this successful mission, he got permission to search for the *Titanic* using the same technology. The *Titanic* was an enormous luxury passenger ship that had been called unsinkable, but on the fifth night of its maiden voyage in April 1912, it hit an iceberg in the North Atlantic and sank. It drifted away from its last known location, and several missions to find it—including a 1977 expedition led by Ballard—came up empty-handed. This "ship of dreams" was lost to the depths for more than 70 years.

It was a challenging expedition: Ballard was looking for the *Titanic* in an area five times the size of New York City. His search for the two submarines gave him an idea for a new search technique. He noticed that ocean currents had created a long chain of debris on the seafloor as the ships sank, so instead of looking for *Titanic*'s hull, he used *Argo*'s sonar to search for a debris chain and its cameras to capture any images from the *Titanic*'s wreckage. *Argo* floated 2.5 miles (4 km) down, just above the seafloor. On September 1, 1985, after more than a week of searching, one of *Titanic*'s boilers—the coal-fired furnaces that powered the ship—appeared on the live video feed. *Argo* continued to stalk the debris trail, and the next day, *Titanic*'s surprisingly intact bow came into view. Still photographs from *Angus*, another unmanned submersible, revealed the ship's hull and mast, including the crow's nest where a lookout, a crewmember who was the eyes of the ship, had first spotted the fatal iceberg. Ballard and his team could see where the ship's grand staircase had once been, and the debris field included perfectly preserved china plates, pairs of shoes, and pieces of furniture. Dozens of scientists—including Ballard, this time inside *Alvin*—would return to the site to study it more thoroughly.

SAVING OUR OCEANS

SAVING OUR OCEANS

Our planet is dependent on the ocean. It plays a huge role in Earth's weather patterns and climate, and it supports an enormous diversity of life from marine mammals to fish, reptiles, and seabirds. The ocean is essential to our survival, partly because its plants and animals are a food source, but also because it provides 70 percent of the oxygen we breathe. The world's oceans face four major threats: global climate change, overfishing, pollution, and habitat destruction. Scientists, conservationists, policymakers, community members, volunteers, and many others are working on ways to combat these threats and keep our oceans—and the marine life they support—healthy.

A CHANGING CLIMATE

Over millions of years, Earth's climate—its weather conditions over a period of many years—has changed many times. Recently, however, Earth's climate has been changing at a much faster rate. Our planet is heating up, and much of this global warming is due to human impact on the environment.

Since the start of the Industrial Revolution in 1760, when humans began to burn fossil fuels like gas, coal, and oil to mass-produce goods such as clothing or to power vehicles, we have been pumping pollutants into Earth's atmosphere. These pollutants, made of gases such as carbon dioxide and other particles, come from the factories and power plants

St. Mark's Square in Venice, Italy, floods with seawater.

that manufacture everything from furniture to toys, and from the cars, trucks, planes, and other gas-powered vehicles and machines we use on a daily basis.

Deforestation—the cutting down of trees to clear the way for farmland, roads, or other human-made spaces—also contributes to climate change. Forests absorb huge amounts of carbon dioxide from the air and release oxygen for us to breathe, similar to the way phytoplankton releases oxygen in the oceans. When large numbers of trees are cut down, they can no longer serve as carbon dioxide "sponges." This leaves more carbon dioxide in the air.

The extra carbon dioxide and other greenhouse gases in the air creates a kind of barrier around our planet. It acts like a big blanket, trapping solar energy, or heat. This trapped heat has caused temperatures across the Earth to rise. Although the Earth does go through natural climate cycles that warm it, the rate at which temperatures are rising is much higher today. The ocean has been getting warmer for more than a hundred years,

but in the past 20 years, the temperature has risen faster than ever before. As temperatures rise, so does the water in our oceans. This is called sea-level rise.

There are two main reasons for sea-level rise. When water heats up, it expands in a process called thermal expansion. This is because the water's molecules increase in

IF ALL THE ICE ON BOTH GREENLAND AND ANTARCTICA MELTED, THE SEA LEVEL WOULD RISE BY 200 FEET (61 M).

volume. Since the same amount of water takes up more space, it can creep up coastlines. Warmer water also leads to warmer air temperatures, which causes ice on land to melt and add more volume to our oceans. The glaciers and ice sheets covering much of Greenland and Antarctica are melting at higher rates. Warmer temperatures have also caused several large icebergs to break off from gigantic ice sheets in recent decades. In 2017 one such iceberg—the size of the state

Deforestation is a major contributor to climate change.

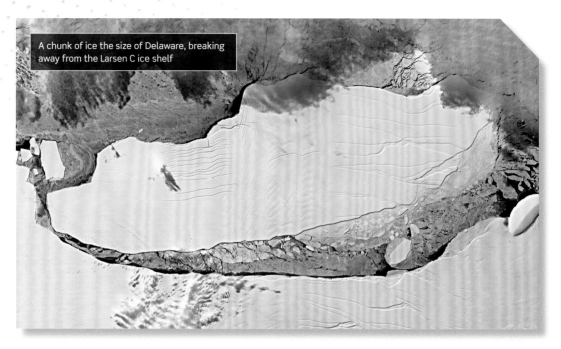

A chunk of ice the size of Delaware, breaking away from the Larsen C ice shelf

of Delaware, U.S.A., and weighing more than a trillion tons—split from an ice sheet in Antarctica.

At our current rate of fossil fuel consumption, which is based on different scenarios, scientists estimate that the warming of the planet could cause sea levels to rise between 10 and 32 inches (26 and 82 cm) by 2100. That could swamp cities at or below sea level, like Venice, Italy, or New Orleans, Louisiana, U.S.A. Many coastal towns and cities have installed systems of floodgates or walls designed to strengthen coastlines and help keep rising waters at bay. These are just preventive measures, though. To help combat global warming and stem rising sea levels, the amount of emissions that each industry or country can produce should be reduced and carefully monitored.

Warmer waters are bad for some marine life. Some coral reefs, for example, have not been able to cope with the warmer temperatures. Remember the small reef-building animals called polyps? They build limestone structures—or coral—to live in, and bacteria

and colorful single-celled algae grow inside them. It's a perfect exchange: The bacteria and algae get a home, and the polyps get food from them. But when water temperatures get too hot, even just by two or three degrees Fahrenheit (1 to 1.7°C), things begin to go wrong. The algae may begin to produce waste that is toxic, or poisonous, to the polyps, so the polyps push the algae out. Without the colorful algae, the corals turn bone white, as if they've been bleached—this is where the term coral bleaching comes from. If the water stays too warm, the polyps can starve to death, creating large barren areas of coral skeletons, but no living coral animals. Scientists are aware of several coral species that have been able to withstand these warmer temperatures, though, and they remain hopeful that more corals will adapt and build new reefs.

OVERFISHING

Fishing provides food for billions of people around the world. And in some places, fresh fish is the major source of protein for the

REPAIRING THE GREAT BARRIER REEF

For three years in a row, the effects of global warming were clearly visible in the Great Barrier Reef. In 2016 and 2017, researchers discovered that higher water temperatures had killed an estimated half of the reef's coral, turning what should look like a kaleidoscope of color into an eerie ghostly white, as shown here. Of the three worldwide mass bleachings of coral reefs that have occurred since 1998, this one was by far the most widespread and damaging. And not only are the reefs themselves threatened, damage to one of the world's largest living structures also affects the hundreds of millions of people who rely on reef fish as their primary food source. It also wreaks havoc on countries that depend on tourism income to fuel local economies.

Scientists noted that reducing greenhouse gas emissions is essential for the future of this global treasure, but other actions can also help keep reefs healthy. These include continued improvement of water quality everywhere, because our rivers and streams make their way to the ocean. Keeping agricultural runoff, pesticides and fertilizers used on farms, from entering the ocean can help corals and the animals that depend on them, including sharks, eels, octopuses ... and us!

A trawl net empties a load of fish.

local population. Over time, however, people have taken some species of fish out of the oceans faster than the fish can reproduce, and the populations of these fish are now lower than what was previously sustainable. This is known as overfishing.

Overfishing was recorded as far back as the early 1800s when whales were targeted for their blubber, used to make oil to light lamps. The overfishing of whales for human uses decimated whale populations. Then, as

the global population of humans grew, so did our need for protein, which meant more pressure on fish. Additionally, technology used to catch fish got better, meaning that boats were able to go farther and catch more fish than ever before. By the mid-20th

century, overfishing became a widespread problem, impacting many fish species.

In certain places, top predatory fish like swordfish, tuna, cod, and sharks have been targeted too heavily for too long. Smaller fish species like sardines, anchovies, and herring are being overfished as well—and many of these smaller fish are caught and turned into pet food. Collectively called forage fish, they travel in large schools of thousands or even millions of fish, a dense, shimmering wall that keeps predators at bay but allows for easy capture of a large number of fish by a giant net. Overfishing forage fish disrupts the food chain. Big fish like salmon and tuna rely on these smaller fish for food. Without little fish to feed on, the big ones go hungry.

Sometimes, key species are targeted for different things. Sharks, for example, are caught for their meat, fins, and liver oil. So shark populations can be devastated by fishers who catch them. Why? Sharks mature

Created in 2012, a shark sanctuary located in the waters off the coast of the Cook Islands in the South Pacific Ocean is one of the largest protected areas for sharks in the world.

slowly and produce few young compared to other fish such as tuna and salmon, which can produce hundreds of thousands of eggs in their lifetime. Fewer sharks in the ocean means fewer chances for reproduction. And fewer shark pups results in a decline in shark populations.

FIXING FISHING

Education, catch quotas (putting limits on the numbers of fish that can be taken), and the creation and maintenance of safe zones for fish to live and breed in are a few ways governments, managers, conservationists, scientists, and others are combating overfishing.

Teaching people to be aware of what they are eating is an important first step. Many experts ask citizens to avoid eating certain kinds of fish that are becoming rare or are important predators that support specific ecosystems. If enough people stop eating certain species, such as Pacific bluefin tuna, then their populations may have time to

rebound. And in the meantime, fishers can focus on trying to catch other, more plentiful species.

Strictly regulating fisheries is a solution that directly addresses the overfishing problem. For example, there are specific regulations about fishing for bluefin tuna in the United States. They can be caught only by using a rod and reel or a hand-thrown harpoon. These fishing techniques prevent large numbers of bluefin tuna from being caught, which helps to keep their populations from declining.

Creating protected areas where fish can feed and reproduce without the threat of being caught is also essential. These safe zones have lots of names—marine sanctuaries, marine managed areas, marine parks, and more—but we'll stick with what they're most frequently called: marine protected areas (MPAs). In nearshore MPAs, for example, marine species can reproduce, and eventually some individuals can swim away from the protected areas to repopulate other areas in the ocean that are used by commercial fishers. This is known as the spillover effect and has been documented to be very effective at keeping certain fish stocks healthy and keeping an ecosystem intact, while still providing food for families outside of protected areas.

There are three main types of MPAs. The first, called fully no-take, prevents fishers from capturing any fish at all. One such MPA, the Papahānaumokuākea Marine National Monument, lies northwest of Hawaii. It was established in 2006 by President George W. Bush. In 2014 President Barack Obama quadrupled its size. It now covers 582,578 square miles (1,508,870 sq km), an area larger than all the national parks in the United States combined. This conservation was a big step toward protecting our vast ocean, as the reserve's waters contain some of the world's healthiest coral reefs. In part because people have never lived on the remote islands and atolls that make up another MPA, the Pacific Remote Islands reserve, the coral reefs found there are pristine, making them an ideal "laboratory" for assessing the effects of climate change in an area largely untouched by humans. The reserve also contains some of the oldest living coral atolls in the world, ancient reefs that have recorded the Earth's climate for thousands of years. These protected waters allow scientists to gain knowledge that can help improve coral reef management in more populated areas of the world.

The second type is a multiple-use MPA. The Great Barrier Reef is a well-known example. Within this zone, people can go boating, diving, and even fishing. But there are controls in place to limit these activities. Specific seasons dictate when fishing is allowed, and certain habitats in these zones are completely off-limits.

SCIENTIST PROFILE

Sylvia Earle

Oceanographer. Conservationist. Explorer. Public speaker. Writer. Film producer. Dr. Sylvia Earle has filled many roles in her pursuit to learn about Earth's ocean and the sea life that inhabits it and to share her discoveries with the world. She has also traveled the globe to lead more than a hundred deep-sea expeditions and logged more than 7,000 hours underwater.

Dr. Earle was one of the first people in marine science to use the Aqua-Lung, equipment developed by Jacques Cousteau and Émile Gagnan, now known as scuba gear. In 1968 she became the first female scientist to leave a submersible underwater to explore the depths free of the vehicle's constraints. Eleven years later, Dr. Earle accomplished one of the deepest untethered dives (she dove without a cable to the surface—just a communication cord connected her to a submersible). She rode to the bottom of the ocean on a submersible and took a two-and-a-half-hour walk on the seafloor—which she said felt more like 20 minutes—earning her the nickname Her Deepness.

Not only is Dr. Earle one of the most fearless divers in history, she is also a tireless advocate of ocean conservation. Under her leadership, the Mission Blue organization seeks to inspire people around the world to explore and protect the ocean. Her goal is to create a global network of "hope spots," or new areas that need protection. By empowering a global network of individuals and communities, Earth's "blue heart" can be protected and restored.

Some protected areas seek to protect a particular type of fish. An example of this species-specific protected area is the bluefin tuna spawning ground in the Gulf of Mexico. It is completely off-limits to fishing so that the tuna can spawn and have a chance to grow. Another example of an area that is used to protect one type of fish is the Cook Islands Shark Sanctuary in the Pacific Ocean. Jess Cramp helped create this 771,000- square-mile (1,997,000-sq-km) safe zone for all sharks and rays, including scalloped hammerheads and great hammerheads (like Finn!), which are endangered throughout the world but still exist in the Cook Islands. Cramp hopes the sanctuary will also help many other vulnerable shark and ray species that live in this area. Within the sanctuary, no commercial boat is allowed to have any sharks onboard, meaning that any shark or ray that is caught as a result of fishing on commercial vessels must be put back. The sale or trade of shark or ray products (including fins, meat, oil, and gill plates) is banned. If sharks or rays are caught in nets meant to catch other fish, fishers are required to return them to the water.

Well-designed MPAs can protect many different species of marine life, including bluefin tuna.

FISHING FOR SOLUTIONS

Although traditional ways of catching fish—with spears, traps, handheld nets, and hook-bearing rods—still exist in some parts of the world today, the rise of commercial fishing in the mid-20th century introduced

SafetyNet designs fishing nets with light-emitting devices like these that attract the fish that fishermen want to catch while repelling bycatch.

Teina Rongo

As a young boy, marine biologist Dr. Teina Rongo spent his childhood fishing on the reefs in the Cook Islands, located in the South Pacific Ocean northeast of New Zealand. But a toxin called ciguatera invaded the reefs—and the fish that swam among them. Ciguatera is found in large reef fish such as trevally and barracuda. These predatory fish eat smaller fish that consume dinoflagellates, a ciguatera-producing marine plankton. People stopped fishing both as a pastime and as an economic necessity, since they didn't want to buy toxin-filled fish. Armed with a doctorate in marine biology, Rongo returned to his childhood fishing grounds to determine what was causing the invasion of ciguatera.

He found that less rainfall creates a saltier ocean—an environment friendly to ciguatera outbreaks. Plus, ciguatera-carrying fish prefer saltier waters. He also believes that disturbances like cyclones clear space for the plankton that produce the ciguatera toxin to establish itself.

Ciguatera is on the decline in the Cook Islands. But will islanders start fishing again? Dr. Rongo believes that if people no longer need to rely on fish for food, they will not return to the islands. If they do need to rely on fish for food and money, islanders will return to fishing as a way of life and target the fish least likely to carry ciguatera. But what about over-fishing? Dr. Rongo is teaching the community, and especially kids, how to fish using sustainable and environmentally friendly methods.

modern fishing methods and at-sea refrigeration, which allow huge numbers of fish to be caught at once. As previously described, this can also be damaging to the ocean ecosystem.

For example, a fishing vessel that uses longlines, a length of line with J-shaped, baited hooks attached at intervals, can have lines coming off of their boat that range from a mile to 62 miles (1.6 to 100 km) long. This method effectively catches the targeted tunas and billfish, but it often causes bycatch, the capture of creatures that the fishers aren't trying to hook. Bycatch can harm or kill animals such as sharks, seabirds, and sea turtles. It can also catch fish that are too small and therefore don't get the chance to spawn a lot to grow their populations. The fishing industry also uses bottom trawls. Boats drag these enormous nets, which can weigh several tons, over the ocean floor. These nets catch everything in their paths. In addition to catching fish, they tear up the seafloor, destroying bottom-dwelling species such as mollusks, sponges, sea urchins, and various worms that burrow into the seabed, as well as deep-sea coral reefs, which grow slowly and cannot recover before trawls plow the area once again.

To reduce unnecessary harm, some fishers are exchanging their J-hooks for circle hooks, which animals like sea turtles are less likely to swallow, and if they do, the circle hook doesn't do as much damage as the J-hook. In some places, it's working: In the Indonesian longline fishery, switching to the less invasive circle hooks reduced sea turtle bycatch by 78 percent, and in the southwest Atlantic longline fishery, circle hooks cut over half of loggerhead and leatherback bycatch. Circle hooks have also significantly reduced the unintended deaths of stingrays, and in Hawaii, they have reduced shark bycatch.

Plastic pollution is one of the biggest threats to the health of the ocean.

Engineers are also developing fishing nets that can save marine life from accidentally getting scooped up by trawls or curtain-like gillnets, which can also be many miles long. For example, SafetyNet is an ocean fishing net that allows certain fish to escape via lighted rings that flash like exit signs to alert smaller fish. The fish can then escape by swimming through the rings. In addition, a panel in the net separates tighter mesh at the top from larger mesh below, allowing bottom-dwelling species such as cod to escape through the bigger holes. In 2011 engineers repurposed fishing lights ordinarily used to attract fish to drive sea turtles away instead. Gillnets are almost invisible underwater,

LESS THAN ONE-FIFTH OF ALL THE PLASTIC IN THE WORLD IS RECYCLED.

which is why sea turtles become ensnared in them. But when lights are attached to nets and set at a wavelength that the turtles can see, they recognize the nets as a "Do Not Enter" zone and cruise by.

Fishers themselves are driving change too. One such fisher designed a squid net that reduces bycatch. The net contains an escape route at its base through which unwanted flounder can flee.

THE PERILS OF PLASTIC

Plastic bags. Soda bottles. Drinking straws. Take-out containers. We live in a world of disposable packaging and single-use (used just one time) plastic items. This is a major problem for our oceans and the marine life that inhabits them. Most plastics don't biodegrade, or completely break down. Instead, over time, sunlight and waves break up plastics into smaller and smaller pieces. About the size of a sesame seed, these little bits are called microplastics. Some are microbeads, which are used in some soaps and toothpastes, and others are pieces from larger plastic items. The United Nations Environment Programme estimates that there could be as many as 51 trillion microplastic particles in the world's oceans—500 times more than the number of stars in our galaxy. Many get concentrated in areas of relatively calm waters that are surrounded by powerful wind-driven surface currents called gyres. Like dogs herding sheep into a central location, the circular motion of the gyre rounds up large amounts of trash into this stable center.

A beach is littered with plastics.

Plastic is trapped within these currents and can take at least 10 years to cycle back out, if it doesn't get eaten by marine life first.

Every year plastic in our oceans kills thousands of marine mammals, seabirds, and fish. Animals get tangled in the plastic and drown, or they swallow it and die because their stomachs cannot process it. Leatherback turtles, for example, often mistake plastic bags for jellyfish—a fatal error. Fish mistake plastic coated in algae for plankton. Many types of plastic also release harmful chemicals when they break down in the ocean. Plastic may absorb pollutants from the water too. These chemicals can build up in the bodies of the animals that eat plastic, and then they can build up in the bodies of animals that eat those animals too. This domino effect can harm the food chain from top to bottom, potentially including humans, who rely on fish and other sea life as a protein source.

TO THE RESCUE

Fortunately, there are solutions to help combat ocean pollution. Every year organizations promote and participate in coastal cleanup days, where people head to beaches and shorelines to pick up plastic and other trash. In 2016 volunteers at the Ocean Conservancy's worldwide coastal cleanup event picked up 18 million pounds (8 million kg) of trash in a single day! But you don't need a yearly event to be helpful. Littering is a major cause of plastic garbage in our oceans, so anytime you see a piece of plastic or trash on the ground or in the water, pick it up and dispose of it properly.

Also, try saying "No, thank you" to single-use plastics such as straws and utensils, which are a source of plastic trash in the oceans. Use a reusable bottle or bring your own bag instead. Many countries, including Myanmar, Bangladesh, and Rwanda, have eliminated plastic bags in supermarkets and

SCIENTIST PROFILE

Anna Cummins and Marcus Eriksen

In 2008, environmental advocates and scientists Anna Cummins, Marcus Eriksen, Ph.D., and Joel Paschal launched the JUNK raft, a vessel built with 15,000 plastic water bottles, to sail across the North Pacific gyre researching and bringing awareness to the plastic pollution problem in the oceans.

Unlike air pollution, which creates a smog that can be easily seen, some 200,000 tons (181,000 t) of plastics caught in the middle of the world's oceans, according to data collected between 2007 and 2013—what Cummins and Dr. Eriksen refer to as "plastic smog"—is harder for people to see. To increase visibility, they co-founded the 5 Gyres Institute, an organization named after the five main gyres around the globe. 5 Gyres conducts research, consults with governments and corporations worldwide, and engages with a global network of ambassadors to stop the flow of plastics into our oceans and environment. They were successful in getting the company Johnson & Johnson to eliminate plastic beads from their soaps.

A simple way to help clean our waters is to participate in local cleanup efforts in your community.

other stores. In 2007 San Francisco, California, was the first city in the United States to ban nonbiodegradable plastic bags, and other cities, such as Boston, Massachusetts, and Portland, Oregon, followed their lead.

These efforts help keep a lot of plastic out of the ocean, but more needs to be done, and organizations such as the nonprofit Sustainable Coastlines are making a positive impact on the health of our ocean. Founded in 2009 by New Zealanders Camden Howitt and Sam Judd, the organization is on a mission to empower communities to look after their local coastlines and waterways. Working as a volunteer for years, Howitt experienced an unforgettable encounter that helped him decide his path. After a beach cleanup in Tonga's Ha'apai Islands, he was freediving alongside a humpback whale and her calf. Howitt was awestruck, and at that moment he decided to quit his day job and dedicate his life to protecting our oceans.

The nonprofit now operates in New Zealand, Papua New Guinea, and Hawaii. In the 10 years since its founding, Sustainable Coastlines has brought together almost 90,000 volunteers to clean up nearly 220 tons (200 t) of trash from coastlines. And they're just getting started!

In addition to developing a litter education curriculum for students and training for teachers, the organization is working alongside New Zealand's government, creating the country's first beach litter database. Sustainable Coastlines is engaging people from all over the country to pick up and count the different types of trash they find along their local coastlines. The volunteers then report their findings to the database, providing real-time information about the problem. With the help of these citizen scientists, and with the goal of continuing to connect communities, business leaders, governments, and scientists, the organization aims to solve the issue of ocean trash pollution longterm. The solutions Sustainable Coastlines

Protecting wetland habitats protects seabird chicks like this limpkin.

creates can be used all around the world. They believe that by working together, we can protect our vast, vital, and beautiful oceans.

HABITAT DESTRUCTION

Sometimes the conditions that plants and animals need to survive change or disappear. For example, a coastal wetland dries up, or a fishing trawler drags a heavy net over deepsea corals, destroying a reef that teems with life. This is habitat destruction, and it impacts ocean and coastal habitats perhaps more than any other areas on Earth.

Estuaries and wetlands are often used as breeding or nursery grounds for ocean animals. Sadly, these areas are the most impacted by habitat destruction. Construction in and near wetlands and swamps; dumping of fertilizer and waste that seeps into the groundwater and then into the sea; dams; fishing; tourism; and climate change all contribute to habitat destruction.

There are people working hard to protect these precious habitats, but there is always more that can be done. Examples include working with communities to better manage resources and even creating new laws that control dumping, construction, fishing, and emissions such as the burning of fossil fuels. Creating MPAs can also be useful in protecting sensitive habitats. These are ways that governments and communities are currently trying to help.

YOU CAN HELP!

Small steps can lead to big changes. Here are some ways you can help keep Earth's ocean healthy.

REDUCE YOUR ENERGY USE

Walk or bike to your friend's house instead of taking the car. Cuddle up in a sweatshirt or catch a breeze through an open window to keep your thermostat from working on overdrive. Turn off the light when you leave a room. Your one carbon footprint makes a difference!

BE PICKY ABOUT PLASTIC

Use reusable bags and bottles. Recycle. Say "No, thank you" to plastic items like straws and utensils that will only be used once. The ocean's animals don't need last year's ice-cream spoon floating in their home. Remind your parents to take bags to the store and try to purchase items that aren't wrapped in plastic.

PROTECT WILDLIFE

Keep that sea star suctioned to its spot in the tide pool. We want everyone to look and explore, but let's let the animals stay in their natural environment. Wildlife is exactly that—wild; it's not meant to be a pet. Stay on marked paths rather than sliding down a sand dune—many little animals and plants call those sandy hills home! Ask your parents to check to make sure the seafood you eat is not threatened. There are great websites such as the Monterey Bay Seafood Watch to help families make delicious and responsible decisions on what to buy.

PLAY WITH CARE

While on a boat, canoe, or kayak, make sure toys, clothes, and trash don't go overboard. On the beach, pick up anything you brought so that these items don't end up in the ocean.

LEARN AND SHARE

The more you know about the ocean and the issues it faces, the more you'll want to help. Be curious and ask a lot of questions! Read, listen, and spread the word—you can teach your friends, family, and neighbors, and the best way to lead is by example. We can all be ocean heroes, no matter where we live!

ABOUT SHARKS PACIFIC AND THE FUTURE

In this book, we reviewed a whole ocean's worth of information. I pull all that knowledge together every day in my job as a scientist and marine conservationist. Despite packing my brain full of information for my work, I still ask a lot of questions and learn new things every single day.

The Cook Islands Shark Sanctuary was created in 2012, after a big team worked for almost two years with the communities to see how they felt about sharks. We learned about the cultural value of sharks to many communities and talked about sharks in fisheries. We discussed the science behind overfishing and we advocated alongside a growing support team for a change in government policy to make the sanctuary possible. I was so proud of the sanctuary and all we did to create this huge area of protected waters for sharks. But I quickly realized it was just a start. There were a number of gaps to fill to ensure that sharks are getting the protection they need—and that the needs and desires of local people are part of the process. That's why I created Sharks Pacific. Our organization combines scientific research with community outreach to understand how people who live in communities in and along the Pacific Ocean interact with sharks, and how to responsibly protect and manage shark populations.

Because we work with government, local communities, and marine life and the ocean, it means that, as part of my job, I do a lot of different things. Depending on the day, I might be in a boat cutting up fish to bait BRUVs (p. 94). I might be talking to fisherman in a harbor about what sharks they've seen. I might be on an industrial fishing boat, riding along so I can tag and release any sharks caught as bycatch. I might be talking with students about what my job entails. Or I might be sitting in front of my computer, logging data and planning more research trips. Research trips are where we get to go into the field and collect valuable data. Here's what one of our trips was like.

THE SHARKIEST PLACE IN THE COOK ISLANDS

The Cook Islands are a group of fifteen islands that make up the whole country. Living in Rarotonga, which is the most populated of the Cook Islands, but which doesn't have a lot of sharks, I heard a lot of stories about sharks on the outer islands. One place in particular kept coming up, an island called Penrhyn. People said that the corals were healthy and teeming with fish life, and that waters there had the most sharks of anywhere in the Cook Islands. But I also learned that some fisherman there were tired of sharks snatching the fish off of their fishing lines before they could reel them in. Several fishermen wanted fewer sharks in the water, and they had started to think about hunting sharks to reduce their numbers.

I wanted to go to Penrhyn to see if it really was the sharkiest place in the Cook Islands, to study the sharks inside and outside of the large lagoon, and to learn more about what the fishermen were dealing with. It took two whole years to raise the funds and find the boat that

A satellite image of Penrhyn's coral atoll

would take the Sharks Pacific team to Penrhyn, which is extremely remote. There are no regularly scheduled ships or flights. Finally, in April 2018, our five-person team climbed aboard a rusty but trusty cargo ship called the *Tiare Taporo* and traveled for seven days to get there. Our long trip was worth it. Penrhyn is one of the most beautiful islands we'd ever seen, with breathtaking views and a colorful, coral-filled lagoon. This is where we would live and do our research for the next month and a half.

One of our research goals was to figure out how many sharks really are in Penrhyn's waters. To do this, we talked to the people of Penrhyn about their sightings and experiences. We also used BRUVs, which recorded more than 140 hours of underwater footage. We had many students from the local Omoka School with us during our BRUVs research; they were great research assistants!

Another important part of our research is how sharks affect people. So we wanted to get to know the people of Penrhyn and how they interact with sharks. We wanted to know what they were seeing, experiencing and feeling, and then figure out how we could help both the sharks *and* the people.

The last part of our research in Penrhyn was tagging sharks. The data we get from doing this helps us better understand where sharks are swimming, and how well shark sanctuaries protect these animals. To tag a shark, first we need to find one. Then we pull it in on a line and attach an identification tag on its dorsal fin. If it's one of the species whose movements we want to track, we will place a satellite tag near the base of its dorsal fin. The sharks swim around with the satellite tags for up to a year. The tag then pops off and transmits the location data to a satellite, which means I can then download the data to my computer. We track the data to

A silvertip reef shark cruises over corals.

form a picture of the shark's movement over time. We can see how far away from the island the shark traveled and also how deep or shallow it swam. We look for any patterns to the data, such as whether the shark is hanging out at a specific spot or whether it makes the same migration routinely.

In Penrhyn, we really wanted to tag two species in particular: oceanic whitetip sharks and silky sharks. These sharks can travel over long distances, so tagging them would help us form a larger picture of how well the shark sanctuary is working. Unfortunately, we didn't find any of these species on this trip. But I couldn't have been prepared for how many sharks we *did* see! We identified whitetip, blacktip, and silvertip reef sharks, as well as dusky sharks. One day, we walked out over a reef to fish for some food and were lucky to catch a delicious-looking dog-tooth tuna. As we were reaching out to grab our dinner, about 50 gray reef sharks came up out of the depths, trying to get the tuna too. It was both fascinating and a little terrifying!

Now, we're analyzing all of the information we collected over our research trip to Penrhyn, which includes watching hours of BRUV footage. The recordings gave us the peek under the surface that we needed. Though we're still reviewing our data, we can already tell that Penrhyn really is the sharkiest place in the Cook Islands—maybe even in all of the South Pacific!

GLOSSARY

Agulhas Current: warm ocean water that moves south along Africa's southeastern coast, through the Indian Ocean

altitude: the distance of something above land

atoll: an island formed by coral

barrier reef: a coral reef separated from shore and running parallel with the land

basin: a dip in the surface of Earth, on land and underwater

break: when a wave curves over and comes apart

bycatch: animals caught accidentally by commercial fishers who are fishing for something else

caldera: a volcanic crater caused by the cone of a volcano caving in, or by huge explosions

Canary Current: movement of cool water through the Atlantic Ocean, driven by the wind and flowing from Africa's East Coast southward and then westward near the Equator

Challenger Deep: the deepest known place in Earth's oceans, located in the Pacific and reaching 36,000 feet (10,980 m) down

cephalopod: a mollusk with jaws and limbs. Squid, octopuses, and nautiluses are examples.

ciguatera: a toxin that poisons fish and people who eat affected fish

circulate: to move in a circular way

Coriolis effect: the impact that Earth's rotation has on how storms and ocean currents move. Storms in the Northern Hemisphere veer right and in the Southern Hemisphere veer left, and currents have looping paths through the ocean.

crest: the peak of a wave

crustacean: an animal with a hard exterior skeleton and jointed legs. A crab is a crustacean.

current: the movement of water between places

cyclone: another name for a hurricane in the South Pacific Ocean. *See* hurricane.

density: how tightly packed a substance's particles are. A ball of ice is heavier than a snowball of the same size because it's more dense. Salt water is more dense than freshwater.

displace: to take the place of something else. For example, a rock dropped into a glass of water displaces the water.

drag: slowed or stopped motion

echinoderm: an animal with a skeleton of fused plates, with tough skin and a circular body. Urchins and sea stars are examples.

ecosystem: a group of organisms and their environment

evaporate: to turn into vapor or fumes

extinction: no longer existing. When all the animals in a species die out, it is extinct.

fossil fuel: coal, oil, or natural gas formed from animal or plant remains in the earth

global ocean conveyor belt: how water circulates around the globe

greenhouse gas: a gas that traps heat in the atmosphere. Carbon dioxide and methane are greenhouse gases.

Gulf Stream: a current of warm water in the Atlantic Ocean

gyre: an area where many currents come together to form a loop

holdfast: a rootlike structure that kelp uses to attach itself to the seafloor.

hurricane: huge ocean storms that occur in the Atlantic Ocean, with devastating weather and powerful winds of more than 74 miles an hour (119 km/h) that rotate around a point of low pressure in the atmosphere. Also called a typhoon or a cyclone, depending on where in the world it occurs.

island: an area of land surrounded by water and smaller than a continent

invertebrate: an animal without a backbone, such as insects and mollusks

jet stream: high-speed and high-altitude atmospheric winds that can reach gusts of 250 miles an hour (402 km/h)

kelp: large seaweeds that can form dense underwater forests

keystone species: a plant or animal that is necessary to keep an ecosystem healthy and balanced

landlocked: surrounded, or nearly surrounded, by land

landmass: a huge area of land, like a continent

mangroves: trees or shrubs in the tropics that form coastal forests

Mariana Trench: an undersea canyon in the Pacific Ocean that contains Earth's deepest depression, Challenger Deep

mariner: a sailor

mass: weight

mid-Atlantic Ridge: a chain of underwater mountains 10,000 miles (16,000 km) long

mollusk: animals with soft bodies and no legs, and often with a shell. Mussels and clams are mollusks.

navigator: a person who makes a course through water or air

ocean: the huge body of salt water that covers about three-quarters of Earth's surface, or any of the bodies of water it is divided into, like the Atlantic Ocean or the Pacific Ocean.

oceanographer: a scientist who studies the oceans, including how deep they are, their water chemistry, ocean physics, marine biology, and the impact of fishing, shipping, and other human activities on the oceans

predator: an animal that hunts other animals for food

prey: an animal that is hunted by other animals

Ring of Fire: an area in the Pacific Ocean dotted with 452 volcanoes and with high volcanic activity. It stretches from the bottom tip of South America, over the West Coast of North America, across the Bering Strait, along Japan and then New Zealand, and it reaches into the Indian Ocean.

rogue wave: a single, unpredictable large open-ocean wave

salinity: the amount of salt in water

sea: a large area at the ocean's edge surrounded by land

seamounts: underwater mountains formed by volcanic activity

storm surge: sea level rise that is caused by changes in atmospheric pressure and storms, and that recedes after the pressure or storm lets up

strait: a narrow waterway that connects two larger bodies of water

subsurface currents: currents in the deeper zones of the ocean that move because of differences in water density

surface currents: currents of water moved mostly by steady winds blowing across the ocean

tradewind: a strong wind that almost always blows in the same direction. Sailors can harness tradewinds to help power their ships.

trench: an underwater canyon formed where an ocean plate slides under continental plate

tropical depression: a storm with winds of less than 39 miles an hour (62 km/h), swirling around an area of low pressure in the atmosphere

tropical storm: a storm with winds between 39 and 73 miles an hour (62 and 118 km/h)

tropical wave: movements of air through the atmosphere that cause heavy rains or strong winds

trough: the low point between wave crests

tsunami: a large wave or series of waves caused by a huge force in the ocean, such as an earthquake

typhoon: another name for a hurricane in the North Pacific Ocean. *See* hurricane.

upwelling: the movement of deep, cold, nutrient-rich water from the seafloor to the ocean's surface

vertebrate: animals with a backbone, including amphibians, birds, fish, and people and other mammals

wave: movement of energy from point to point, or the swell of water as it rises

zooplankton: small organisms, such as larvae and one-celled organisms, floating near the ocean's surface that eat phytoplankton and other zooplankton

INDEX

Boldface indicates an illustration or image.

IMAGE CREDITS

All illustrations by Ben Shannon,
except as noted:

Back Jacket Flap: Andy Mann;
1, divedog/SS; 6 (UP) Andy Mann,
(CTR) Kirby Morejohn, (LO) Jess
Cramp; 7, Kirby Morejohn; 10, NG
Maps; 11, Harvepino/SS; 12, NASA;
13 (UP) Dawnyh/DT, (LO) Hoberman
Collection/UIG/GI; 14, Anton_
Ivanov/SS; 15, Rosenstiel School
of Marine and Atmospheric Science
at the University of Miami; 16,
Alberto Loyo/SS; 17 (CTR) Everett
Historical/SS, (LO) NG Maps; 18 (UP)
Sergey Novikov/SS, (LO) Nattika/SS;
19, Sergey Novikov/SS; 22,
Flystock/SS; 23, ohrim/SS; 24 (UP)
Hero Images/GI, (LO) Dallas Reeves/
SS; 26, Sky Cinema/SS; 27, Becky
Starsmore/SS; 28, José Antonio
Peñas/SCI; 29, Capt. Roger Wilson/
NOAA National Weather Service
Collection; 32, NG Maps; 33 (UP)
Everett Historical/SS, (LO) Kevin
Schafer/ASP; 34 (UP LE) Perception
of Reality/SS, (UP RT) Estate of
Marie Tharp and Lamont-Doherty
Earth Observatory; 35, NG Maps;
36, NG Remote Imaging; 37 (UP)
Akshay-PhotOvation/SS, (LO) Dmitrij
Skorobogatov/SS; 40, Walter E.
Harvey/SCI; 41 (UP) Yevgen Belich/
SS, (LO) Ferenc Cegledi/SS;
42, Ethan Daniels/SS; 43, Dee
Browning/SS; 44 (UP) divedog/SS,
(LO) Solvin Zankl/ASP; 45, Helmut
Corneli/ASP; 46, © David Gruber; 47
(UP) Courtesy of Expedition to the
Deep Slope 2007, NOAA-OE, (LO)
Ocean Networks Canada; 50 (LO LE)
Pete Niesen/SS, (LO RT) Tyler Fox/
SS; 51 (UP) Ethan Daniels/SS, (LO)
Todd Walsh © 2014 MBARI; 52, Dr. D.
P. Wilson/SCI; 53 (dugong) Norbert
Probst/GI, (reef) JC Photo/SS, (fish)
Pete Niesen/SS; 54, AshtonEa/SS;
55 (UP LE) Brett Seymour / National
Park Service, (UP RT) Vinay Udyawer;
56, Alexander Mazurkevich/SS; 57,
worldswildlifewonders/SS; 58, Joe
Dovala/GI; 59, Danita Delimon/GI;
62, Achimdiver/SS; 63, PJ photogra-
phy/SS; 64, WaterFrame/ASP;
65, Gecko1968/SS; 66 (UP LE)
MZPHOTO.CZ/SS, (UP RT)
Goncaloferreira/DT; 67, Hemis/ASP;
68, Wet Lizard Photography/SS; 69,
Amilevin/DT; 70, Stocktrek Images,
Inc./ASP; 71, Richard Whitcombe/
SS; 72 (UP) Ethan Daniels/SS, (LO)
DaveBluck/IS; 73 (LO LE) David
Evison/SS, (LO RT) NatureDiver/SS;
74, Danté Fenolio/SCI; 75 (UP)
Gerald and Buff Corsi/Visuals
Unlimited, Inc./GI, (LO) Ocean
Networks Canada / Canadian
Scientific Submersible Facility
(CSSF/ROPOS); 78 (LO LE) Allison
Bronson/AMNH, (LO RT) Kelly
Matsunaga; 79, James St. John;
80, Sergey Uryadnikov/DT; 81, Tom
McHugh/SCI; 82, Nina B/SS; 83,
Michael Maier / Barcroft USA /
Barcroft Media via GI; 84, W. Scott
McGill/SS; 85 (UP) Gerard Soury/GI,
(LO) wildestanimal/SS; 86, Shane-
Gross/IS; 87(UP) bearacreative/SS,
(LO) Krzysztof Odziomek/SS; 88,
Jamiegodson/DT; 89 (UP) Bill
Curtsinger/GI, (LO) Angel Simon/SS;
92, The Natural History Museum,
London/SCI; 93 (UP) Claus Lunau/
SCI, (LO) B. Murton/Southampton
Oceanography Centre/SCI; 94,
ultramarinfoto/IS; 95 (UP) Danita
Delimont/ASP, (LO) Bettmann/GI;
96, PA Images/ASP; 97, OAR/NURP/
Woods Hole Oceanographic Inst.;
98 (LO LE) B. Murton/Southampton
Oceanography Centre/SCI; (LO RT)
Shmulik Blum; 99, Emory Kristof/
NGC; 102, irisphoto1/SS; 103, KPG
Payless2/SS; 104, NASA; 105, Rich
Carey/SS; 106, AlenaLitvin/SS;
107, Joshua Beniston/SS; 108,
© Stuart Pearce; 109, SafetyNet
Technologies Ltd; 110, Dr. Teina
Rongo; 111, Rich Carey/SS; 112,
Ryan Martin for 5 Gyres Institute;
113 (both) 5 Gyres Institute; 114,
seamind224/SS; 115, Kristin
Howell/SS; 116 (TOP TO BTM)
FatCamera/IS, Janine Lamontagne/
IS, Darilynn/SS, BlueOrange Studio/
SS, Tropical studio/SS

RESOURCES

BOOKS

Doubilet, David, and Jennifer Hayes. *Face to Face with Sharks*. National Geographic Kids, 2009.

Hague, Bradley. *Alien Deep: Revealing the Mysterious Living World at the Bottom of the Ocean*. National Geographic Kids, 2012.

Musgrave, Ruth. *Everything Sharks: All the Shark Facts, Photos, and Fun That You Can Sink Your Teeth Into*. National Geographic Kids, 2011.

Nicklin, Flip, and Linda Nicklin. *Face to Face with Whales*. National Geographic Kids, 2010.

Rizzo, Johnna. *Ocean Animals: Who's Who in the Deep Blue*. National Geographic Kids, 2016.

Skerry, Brian. *Face to Face with Manatees*. National Geographic Kids, 2010.

Skerry, Brian, Elizabeth Carney, and Sarah Wassner Flynn. *Ultimate Book of Sharks: Your Guide to These Fierce and Fantastic Fish*. National Geographic Kids, 2018.

Swanson, Jennifer. *Absolute Expert: Dolphins: All the Latest Facts from the Field*. National Geographic Kids, 2018.

Swanson, Jennifer. *Astronaut-Aquanaut: How Space Science and Sea Science Interact*. National Geographic Kids, 2018.

Wilsdon, Christina. *Ultimate Oceanpedia: The Most Complete Ocean Reference Ever*. National Geographic Kids, 2016.

WEBSITES

NASA's Climate Kids
climatekids.nasa.gov/menu/ocean/

National Geographic Kids Oceans Portal
kids.nationalgeographic.com/explore/ocean-portal/

National Geographic Oceans Page
nationalgeographic.com/environment/oceans/

NOAA Ocean Activities and Resources for Kids
oceanservice.noaa.gov/kids/

More About Sharks Pacific
sharkspacific.org

More About Sustainable Coastlines
sustainablecoastlines.org

More About the Thresher Shark Project
threshersharkproject.org

Science SUPERHEROES

CHECK OUT MORE SCIENCE SUPERHEROES!

Tomecek, Steve. *Dirtmeister's Nitty Gritty Planet Earth*. National Geographic Kids, 2015.

Ehlmann, Bethany. *Dr. E's Super Stellar Solar System*. National Geographic Kids, 2018.

Green sea turtles swim in the warm waters off the coast of Hawaii.

Acknowledgments

The publisher wishes to thank the book team: Priyanka Lamichhane, Julide Dengel, Sarah J. Mock, Mike McNey, Joan Gossett, Anne LeongSon, Gus Tello, Michelle Harris, and Girl Friday Productions. The publisher would also like to thank Kathryn Williams for her writing contribution to the book.

Since 1888, the National Geographic Society has funded more than 12,000 research, exploration, and preservation projects around the world. The Society receives funds from National Geographic Partners, LLC, funded in part by your purchase. A portion of the proceeds from this book supports this vital work. To learn more, visit natgeo.com/info.

For more information, visit nationalgeographic .com, call 1-800-647-5463, or write to the following address:

National Geographic Partners
1145 17th Street N.W.
Washington, D.C. 20036-4688 U.S.A.

Visit us online at nationalgeographic.com/books

For librarians and teachers: ngchildrensbooks.org

More for kids from National Geographic: natgeokids.com

National Geographic Kids magazine inspires children to explore their world with fun yet educational articles on animals, science, nature, and more. Using fresh storytelling and amazing photography, *Nat Geo Kids* shows kids ages 6 to 14 the fascinating truth about the world—and why they should care. kids.nationalgeographic.com/subscribe

For information about special discounts for bulk purchases, please contact National Geographic Books Special Sales: specialsales@natgeo.com

For rights or permissions inquiries, please contact National Geographic Books Subsidiary Rights: bookrights@natgeo.com

Library of Congress Cataloging-in-Publication Data

Names: Levit, Joseph, author. | Cramp, Jessica, author.
Title: Captain Aquatica / by Joe Levit with Jessica Cramp.
Description: Washington, DC : National Geographic Kids, 2019. | Audience: Age 8-12. | Audience: Grade 4 to 6.
Identifiers: LCCN 2018031318| ISBN 9781426332920 (pbk.) | ISBN 9781426332937 (hardcover)
Subjects: LCSH: Ocean--Juvenile literature.
Classification: LCC GC21.5 .L49 2019 | DDC 551. 46--dc23
LC record available at https://lccn.loc.gov/ 2018031318

Printed in China
19/RRDS/1